LONDON
DAWN *to* DUSK
CELEBRATION OF A CITY

JENNY OULTON

PHOTOGRAPHS BY

DAVID PATERSON

Jenny Oulton

FOREWORD BY

JOHN HUMPHRYS

NEW HOLLAND

Contents

First publis

London • C

10 9 8 7 6

24 Nutford

80 McKenz

Level 1/Un

218 Lake R

Copyright ©
Copyright ©
Copyright ©

ISBN 1 859

Publishing M
Project Edito
Editors: Vic S
Designer & C
Production: J
Index: Janet I
Editorial Assi

Reproduction
Printed and b

Introduction

*L*ondon's existence spans almost exactly the two thousand years of Christianity which the Millennium has lately marked. Twenty centuries have left their imprint on the city's shape, its architecture and the daily lives of those who live, work or simply enjoy themselves there. *London: Dawn to Dusk* celebrates this 'Flower of Cities All' by tracing its day (which in truth never ends) against an enthralling backcloth embroidered, like few others, with golden strands of history.

It is impossible to walk round London without coming upon, amongst the immediately modern, some corner of Roman, Tudor, Georgian or Victorian London. A little piece preserved by chance or design. Who would expect to find, dwarfed by the high rise office blocks on the Euston Road, a perfect row of Georgian shops or just outside Tower Hill tube station a great fragment of the Roman wall that surrounded the City of Londinium? Turn down an alleyway off a busy thoroughfare and an older age is revealed at every turn (the lanes, courts and lawyers' chambers of The Temple, off Fleet Street, are luminous examples). This infinite variety is what this book hopes to explore.

London means different things to different people. Native Londoners take it for granted. It is where they live and work. They grumble at its inconveniences and ignore its opportunities. They moan about pollution, traffic, the overcrowding on the tubes and irregularity of the buses. They complain of expense, of bad government, of poor services. Yet remove them from its roaring heart and they feel diminished and return with a sense, only half recognised, of coming home.

For the Londoner by adoption and its multitude of visitors it is a wonderful place of theatres, concert halls, art galleries, museums and festivals. A place which for hundred of years has been a mecca to all who wanted to reach the top of their particular tree. In every field of work, London acts as a magnet: in

Sun-up in Regent's Park. Within the wide, open spaces here can be found London Zoo, a popular boating lake, an open-air theatre and the lovely Queen Mary's Rose Garden. The park was named after the Prince Regent (later King George IV) and it was intended that a new palace for him would be housed in its centre. Happily, the palace was never built, so Regent's Park is a park for the people.

The Queen's House, Greenwich, as seen from Greenwich Park looking north across the river to the Isle of Dogs. This little jewel of a house, the first Palladian building in England, was designed by Inigo Jones in 1613. Today it is open to the public – one of three museums in Greenwich Park.

government, the arts, in law, in business. London is not only the capital city and therefore the administrative centre of the country, it is also the centre for almost everything else. The City of London is the financial centre of the country and one of the biggest international money markets in the world. Almost all large British companies and huge numbers of foreign companies feel the need to have a base in the capital.

From its first creation under the Romans two thousand years ago, London has had a life of its own and has grown and developed with little formal planning. While sometimes this has been a disadvantage, it is also one of the strengths of the metropolis.

Unlike many planned cities, London has always had the capacity to change to suit the needs of each generation, and it has changed many times. Some change has been enforced: the Great Fire of 1666 left virtually the whole of the City of London in ashes, the bombing of the Second World War made thousands homeless and left much of the city a desolate sea of rubble. The demands of the populace meant that in both cases London was quickly rebuilt. It has been rebuilt again and again. The present ground level is twenty feet above Roman London. The wonder is that with so much rebuilding over the centuries, an astonishing amount of the old still survives.

For anyone approaching retirement age after a lifetime spent in London, the changes have been staggering. To those growing up after the war, the city was a drab, battered place, but one that

Canada Water is one of the recent Jubilee Line Stations. The extension to the Jubilee Line of London's underground railway system has brought previously distant suburbs within easy reach of the centre of town. Many of the stations have been designed by celebrated architects and there are those who travel on the line just to admire the contemporary structures.

afforded vivid images to film-makers with its bomb-sites dressed in London Pride and valerian and its buildings blackened by centuries of soot. And London in the fog. The 'Peasouper'– a constant hazard of the post war years – is now a thing of the past. To experience the smog was less than pleasant. To find oneself marooned in the middle of the road without having any knowledge of having left the pavement was at best scary, at worst actually dangerous. The smog entered homes, hospitals, theatres; a performance at Sadlers Wells was cancelled because the audience could not see the stage; a bus travelling from Leicester Square to Tottenham could only make

the journey with a cyclist riding in front wearing a white scarf; a fire engine crawled to a fire with a man walking in front with a flare to light the way. Smog was caused by the smoke from a million chimneys, industrial and domestic; coal fuelled the Industrial Revolution, warmed and powered London, helping to turn it into the great seat of Empire; Seacoal Lane, close to Ludgate Circus, is an echo of the medieval wharf on the Fleet river, where the coal was landed. Well within recent memory, 'flatties', colliers from the Tyne were a common sight along the Thames as they made their way to riverside power stations like Battersea, burning the coal which powered industry and heated every home. Now it is forbidden to burn smoking fuel and London is a cleaner city. But, although the smogs are no more, there are still times when the Thames is swathed in mist and the lights of Westminster glimmer romantically through it as they did for Turner and Monet and Monet's friend Whistler.

In the last fifty years whole districts have been transformed. The most dramatic change of all has occurred in Docklands. Thirty years ago the Docks were thriving, employing a vast work force. Within a few years they were derelict, machines making redundant the tough and independent London docker. The area became an employment black spot with the majority of the population out of work. Now a huge transformation has been wrought. Docklands has become one of the commercial centres of London full of magnificent office blocks, fine modern housing, new schools, shops, colleges, hotels and sporting facilities. What was, just a few years ago, a contaminated, heavily polluted area is now a haven for wildlife. The docks are full of fish and the skies above with birds. The Isle of Dogs is rapidly becoming a rival to the City of London (the 'Square Mile') as firms from all over the world move into a 21st-century environment. Dominating this new 'city' is the Canary Wharf Tower, huge like the giant stump of a carpenter's pencil; obliquely across the Thames, its mass is challenged by the huge

Green Park has few flowers,
other than spring bulbs,
but plenty of grass and trees.
Some say this lack of flowers
is because in the Middle Ages
it was a burial ground for
lepers. The Tyburn, one
of the underground rivers
of London, runs through the
park below the grass and can
be heard from the centre.

white arc of the (temporary?) Millennium
Dome, both done down in elegance by Wren's
riverside architecture at Greenwich.

Docklands lies due east of the city's ancient
heart; equidistant in the west is its utter contrast,
the Royal Borough of Kensington, where another
sort of change has taken place. After the Second
World War it was a place of dark residential hotels
full of genteel, maiden ladies living lives of
unblemished respectability and worshipping at St
Mary Abbots. Each had her own table in her hotel
dining room, with her own pots of jam and mar-
malade, put out each day for her and only her use.

Here, young nephews and nieces took tea with
the aged relatives, and sat up straight and were
careful to say please and thank you. Now those
ladies have gone as have their hotels. Kensington
today is bursting with young and vividly cosmopolitan life and is so transformed that it is
almost impossible to remember how it felt in the
1950s. Docklands and Kensington are just two
illustrations of what has happened in recent years.
There are dozens of others.

What excitement London holds for children!
Some pleasures have been enjoyed for generations.
There is the wonder of Christmas; the lights, the

A hot summers day in St James's Park. Today the park can be enjoyed by everyone, but when it was first laid out in 1532 by Henry VIII and later, under the Stuart kings, it was used only by the court. It has a delightful lake which is home to waterfowl found nowhere else in London.

shop windows in all their finery, the Christmas plays and pantomimes. Or the thrill of climbing the Dome of St Paul's Cathedral for the first time; the sense of danger, of vertigo, of exhaustion coupled with elation, when with shaking legs the small visitor reaches the Golden Gallery on top and looks over the huge expanse of the city. This is a centuries' old pleasure. Some childhood delights are now sadly too dangerous for the modern child. Forty years ago the streets of London were giant playgrounds. Children rode their bikes and scooters around the residential areas, performing 'no hand' stunts. Today the volume of traffic would render such sports suicidal. But there are compensations. London is full of adventure parks and indoor spaces with climbing frames and rope ladders and long tubes to crawl through. Every museum has special activities for children where they can find monsters in paintings or learn to write their names in hieroglyphs, even call up knowledge on a computer screen. Something is lost, but something else has taken its place. There are new pleasures too. It is only in the last few years that it has been possible to walk along the river from Tower Bridge to Canary Wharf, have lunch on a Chinese junk moored in

ABOVE This is a view of Trafalgar Square that few people will be awake to see: it is early morning and the fountains have yet to be turned on. The lovely old building, the National Gallery, is reflected in the still waters of the basin. The square will not look so clean and enticing again until the next morning.

LEFT The clock tower of the Palace of Westminster is familiarly named after its bell, 'Big Ben'. The bell weighs over 13½ tonnes and was cast in Whitechapel in 1858. It was brought to Westminster through crowd-lined streets on an open cart pulled by 16 horses. The chimes of Big Ben are used to introduce newscasts throughout the country and to herald the start of each new year.

RIGHT The City of London seen across the Thames from Hays Wharf. Much of the City was bombed during the Second World War, especially along the riverside. Since the War there has been much rebuilding – some structures being rebuilt more than once in the last 50 years.

the old docks, and return by the driverless Dock-lands Light Railway. It is this ability to change, to recreate itself for each generation, that makes London a great city.

Each season holds its own delights; the bright promise of spring in the parks, the cafe society of long summer days, the wonderful freshness in the air and bronzing of leaves in autumn and the bright crispness of cold winter days.

But the changes this book will explore are the changes that take place over a single day: from dawn to dusk. Very early in the morning, just as the sun makes its first appearance London seems empty. The few who may be abroad feel that it is theirs alone. The streets glisten with their morning wash and the air smells fresh and new.

This impression is swiftly lost as London comes to life and fills and work begins. First the City and the new, gleaming business centre of Canary Wharf, to which much of the national press has

A view of Buckingham Palace without crowds of people taking photographs is a rare sight indeed. It is early in the morning and the sentries have yet to take up their positions in the boxes behind the railings. The only human figures in sight are the bronze statues on the left and the right, which stand at the base of the Queen Victoria Monument.

moved from its historic home in Fleet Street; the money men are taken in sleek lifts to their high offices to begin contacting their colleagues in the money markets of the East. Their day of high tension and drama, dealing in vast sums of money or commodities, starts early. A little later it is the turn of the West End as shops, both great and small, prepare to open their doors to the public.

By mid-morning the whole metropolis is alive and throbbing. Tourists pour into Westminster Abbey, St Paul's, the Tower of London. Photographs are taken of the Houses of Parliament and Big Ben. The Guard is changed at Buckingham Palace. As the sun climbs to its height, Trafalgar Square fills with people feeding the pigeons, with children sitting on the lions.

At lunch time the streets of the business areas are crammed with workers taking a midday break. More and more, in recent years, London has

become a city of the outdoors; lunch, weather permitting, is taken sitting on the grass in the parks or squares, or at the small cafés and pubs which sport tables on the pavement. In the afternoon, the weary tourist may seek the less crowded museums, the quieter treasures of London – the Wallace Collection, the Courtauld Institute Galleries, the Geffrye Museum. They may enjoy a concert in one of the Royal Parks, or a matinee at the new Globe Theatre. Or they may take a boat down the river to visit Greenwich or upstream to Kew Gardens and Hampton Court. They may visit the London Planetarium and relax while the wonders of the heavens are revealed above them.

As evening approaches, there is the grand exodus as the workers go home to the suburbs, pouring into the Underground and railway stations or piling onto buses. Some will seek a 'happy hour' drink, and the pubs are briefly overflowing. As night falls, it is the restaurants which do the best trade. Theatre or concert goers dine before the evening's entertainment. The West End lights up as theatres and cinemas advertise their attractions and stars in multi-coloured neon. Shaftesbury Avenue, Covent Garden, Piccadilly Circus and Leicester Square are crammed with people ready to have a good night out.

Now London is floodlit. Few sights are more magical than Thames-side's famous buildings rising out of the darkness across the water. Later, as the theatres empty, London becomes the preserve of the really dedicated pleasure seeker. The nightclubs, casinos, gambling clubs and drinking clubs come into their own. These revellers may not go home until the night is far gone, dawn once more breaks over the great old city and the whole daily cycle of life starts over again.

'Dear God! the very houses seem asleep;
and all that mighty heart is lying still!'
WILLIAM WORDSWORTH

As Morning Breaks

*I*n London, dawn is best enjoyed in the spring and summer months. In the short days of winter the city has already come alive by sunrise and dawn goes unnoticed, but in the summer, when few people are about, it has a mysterious other life. There is a feeling of newness. The light is soft and clear, the air fresh. The streets glisten from their early watering. There is almost a silence, apart from the quiet hum of early traffic, a tangible sense that life is about to begin anew.

But this is only an impression – because, in reality, London never stops. Look up at any office building early in the morning and you will almost certainly see cleaners already at work, preparing the building for the daytime staff, who are probably still abed; late into the night the newspapermen have put their last editions to bed, hospitals have treated the casualties of too good a time, the police have dealt with revellers who have over-revelled, the homeless have settled in doorways in their sleeping-bags and party-goers have taken cabs home after a night of dancing and gambling in West End clubs. Already the greengrocers, fishmongers and butchers will have bought their day's supplies at the great old markets and some of the more specialized antique markets will have been trading busily, dealer to dealer.

Dawn Traders

*L*ondon's trade markets are busy when most of the city is asleep. Goods arrive soon after midnight and trading is done in the early hours of the morning. By the time most people are waking up, traders have completed their business and are enjoying a well-earned meal and a drink in a market pub.

The great trade markets of Smithfield, Billingsgate and Covent Garden deal as wholesalers, providing the food necessary to feed a burgeoning city. The

When the first Palace of Westminster was built in the 1050s it stood on an island. As the sky begins to lighten over the present Houses of Parliament the building still looks isolated, an illusion that will quickly be shattered as the seat of British Government comes to life.

A Portobello Road dealer enjoys the warm, early-morning sun. She will be here every Saturday, whatever the weather, throughout the year. Most of the traders deal in small antique goods that are easily transported, and attend several different markets each week, spending a lot of their time setting up and dismantling their displays.

Borough Market in Southwark, which almost certainly descends from the market held on old London Bridge in the Middle Ages, provides an outlet for the fruit and vegetable farmers of Kent. Smithfield, across the river, stands on what was an open space – 'Smoothfield' – just outside the city walls. From the 12th to the 19th century, regular horse and cattle markets were held here, and live cattle were driven to market, 'on the hoof' through the streets of London. At one time as many as 700,000 beasts visited the market each week. Now it is a 'dead meat' market, with its own grand market hall designed by Horace Jones in the 1860s, where butchers gather to obtain their daily supplies. Billingsgate fish market, now moved downstream from its site in the heart of the city to Docklands, is perhaps London's oldest market, having originated in

Saxon times, while Covent Garden, the famous fruit and vegetable market begun in 1670, is the youngest of the wholesale markets. Like Billingsgate, it has been moved to a new location miles away, at Nine Elms.

The antique markets are also for early risers: most are busy by 9am, although trading begins while the stalls are being set up. Portobello Road is the most famous and popular of all the antique markets. Antique shops line the street, but it comes to life on Saturdays, when stalls selling every imaginable 'collectable' are set up. Long before the public begin to arrive, the dealers will have been buying from one another. A desirable piece may change hands three or four times, making its way from stall to stall, the price rising a little each time and, by the time it is finally carried away by a satisfied 'punter', it may cost as much as 100 per cent

more that it did two hours earlier. At the other end of Portobello Road, another market, selling mainly fruit and vegetables to locals, flourishes several days a week.

Columbia Road wears two dresses: drab everyday overalls and bright Sunday best. Every Sunday morning this East End street is banked with parallel lines of stalls selling trays of petunias, pansies, lobelias and begonias, mountains of house plants and cut flowers and avenues of young trees. Eager London gardeners throng down the middle, vying with one another to find the finest plants. Arrive early for the best specimens, or late to pick up bargains, as traders pile tray upon tray to sell two, three, or four for the price of one. So successful has Columbia Road become that Londoners think nothing of travelling 30 kilometres (about 20 miles) or more for a chance to restock their

ABOVE AND LEFT Anyone who loves flowers will love Columbia Road Market. Mostly devoted to plants and seedlings, it also has stalls of cut flowers on sale at reasonable prices, as can be seen above. When the market is at its busiest it is almost impossible to move down the centre of the road.

This is not the place to come for the rare or the exotic, but the more common flowers and shrubs can be found here in abundance. This truly is the market for everyone who loves gardening but has a limited budget, although it is not easy sticking to a budget when surrounded by the plenty on display!

BELOW Petticoat Lane Market, which functions on Sunday mornings, got its name from the second-hand clothes that have been sold here since the 16th century. The market was given added impetus by the Jewish immigrants of the 18th and 19th centuries. Today, in addition to old clothes, it is possible to buy all sorts of household goods, both in Middlesex Street, where the main market stands, and in the surrounding roads. Don't expect many bargains though.

gardens, enjoy the kaleidoscope of colour and exchange tips with fellow enthusiasts.

The shops in the neighbourhood also help to feed the English passion for growing things, and sell all manner of gardening goods including urns, statues, terracotta pots, garden furniture, decking and tiles. There are lorries selling bags of manure and compost from their tailgates and, for the weary shopper laden with packages, there are cafés selling refreshments: croissants, bagels stuffed with cream cheese and smoked salmon, or home-made carrot and fruit cakes. The cafés are tiny, so people spill out, adding to the crowds

in the street, perching with their coffee on any vacant bit of wall or sitting on the pavement. By lunch-time it is all over: the remaining plants are packed away and Columbia Road returns to its weekday look.

Brixton – a Splash of Colour

London's street markets – and there are dozens of them dotted round the inner and outer suburbs selling general goods, crafts, antiques, books, clothes, furniture or plants – are an up-to-date urban echo of the medieval market town. They are no longer essential to the lives of the communities they serve but simply widen the choices available to the shopper and add colour to the neighbourhood.

People shop in markets because they are cheap, colourful and fun. Here, the cockney or Rastafarian banter can be heard at its spontaneous best. Despite the greater convenience of supermarkets, the sheer humanity of the street market gives it a quality that the most super of superstores will never possess.

Every part of London has at least one general goods market reflecting the needs of the local population. None demonstrates this better than Brixton Market in south London. The Brixton population is an exotic mixture of West Indians, Maltese, Chileans, Cypriots, Asians, Vietnamese and, despite impressions to the contrary, over 60 per cent native British. Brixton first developed as a smart residential area for city gents and their families, and for a while was known as the 'Belgravia of the South'. With the coming of the railway, wealthier residents were able to move further afield and more and more building development of the humbler kind led to an influx of the lower-paid 'working classes'. The larger properties became boarding-houses, where many music-hall performers had lodgings, among them Dan Leno and Fred Karno and, famously in recent times, the child John Major, whose father was a circus and music-hall artiste.

Brixton Market started in the 19th century,

There could hardly be a greater contrast between Brixton Market (right) and Leadenhall Market (below). Brixton serves its lively multi-ethnic community with cheap and colourful produce piled high on each stall, while all is discretion in the ancient City market of Leadenhall, with its elegant arcading and small shops. The market, which stands on the site of the Roman market, or forum, dates back to the 14th century, although the present building is Victorian. On sale at Leadenhall each weekday are meat, game and other provisions, as well as coffee and croissants.

with the main market under the railway arches lining Electric Avenue (so called because it was one of the first streets in London to be lit by electricity). A threat of closure in the 1950s was scotched by a petition which showed that customers came from miles around to enjoy its fairground atmosphere and eccentric characters. On sale among the general goods today are exotic fruit and vegetables. A few years ago, many Londoners would have looked askance at sweet potatoes, chillies, peppers, okra, mangoes, squashes and watermelons. Ethnically diverse Brixton Market and others like it in London have opened new culinary doors to the British and these 'strange fruits' can now all be found in the average supermarket. But Brixton Market is wonderfully cheap. A pound coin might, on a good day, buy one avocado pear in Belgravia. In Brixton it might buy ten.

PRECEDING PAGES At dawn the wildfowl have the Round Pond in Kensington Gardens to themselves. The gardens were once the private grounds of Kensington Palace. King George I planned the pond and the Broad Walk, while Queen Caroline, wife of George II, was largely responsible for how the gardens look today.

Preparations for a New Day

While early-morning market stalls are being set up all over London, the post-man, the newspaper boy and the milkman start making deliveries to still-sleeping residents in the city's suburbs. Light sleepers will already have been woken by the dawn chorus created by capital's birds marking out their territories with melodious song.

For those who like early mornings best, hun-dreds of fitness clubs all over London open early, allowing dedicated health buffs to pump iron or swim before work. For those who must swim in the open, there is the Serpentine Lake in Hyde Park or Highgate Ponds on Hampstead Heath, where a few eccentrics can be seen every day, whatever the weather, flinging themselves into the icy water. A Christmas Day plunge is an annual ritual for many of the tougher spirits. Some ener-

Regent's Park covers some 190 hectares (472 acres) and, deserted at dawn, looks like the grounds of a great country estate. Originally known as Marylebone Park, it was used by King Henry VIII as a hunting park. In 1812 it was laid out in its present form, as a 'garden suburb', by the Prince Regent's architect John Nash.

getic souls will take advantage of the unlocking of the park gates at dawn to go jogging or roller-blading, or will take their dogs for the first of their daily walks.

During the hours of darkness the parks and the heaths have been the preserve of London's wildlife. Urban foxes, which grow in number each year in the parks of Central London and are to be found scavenging in all the more leafy suburbs, will now disappear to sleep the day away. Squirrels

will increase their vigilance as they forage for nuts and berries and the cockney sparrows and pigeons will gather in the hope of an early meal from some old lady with a bag of stale bread.

The best places to be at sunrise on a fine summer's day are the open spaces and wide streets of the capital. Go to Whitehall or to Trafalgar Square, where the dramatic shadow of Nelson's Column is cast the length of the square. Or to the Mall, and the quiet of St James's Park and Green

ABOVE Hampstead and
Highgate are connected by a
large area of open heathland,
of which Parliament Hill is
the most southerly point. The
hill, at 97 metres (319 feet),
is not particularly high, but
nevertheless offers wonderful
views. The name may
originate from the time of
the Gunpowder Plotters who,
so it is said, planned to meet
here to watch Parliament
blow up in 1605.

RIGHT John Nash was
responsible for the grand
overall design for the
development around Regent's
Park, but some of the terraces
were designed by other
builders and architects.
Cornwall Terrace, with its
elegant neoclassical design
and fine pediment, is the
work of Decimus Burton.

RIGHT Sloane Square is unusual for London in that it is paved rather than landscaped. It has an almost Parisian look, an air of sophistication that befits one London's most expensive and fashionable districts. The sculpture on the fountain, which features a naked damsel emptying her water pots into the surrounding pool, is by Gilbert Ledward and dates from 1953.

BELOW Ornaments and statues adds to the pleasures that many of London's parks have to offer. This fine stone maiden is to be found in Kensington Gardens.

Park. Here, glimpses may be caught of the early-morning exercise of the Household Cavalry as they go through their paces, each trooper riding one horse and controlling another alongside. Occasionally, one of the carriages and horses of the royal household can be seen trotting up the Mall as the horses are schooled in good behaviour prior to a state visit, for which they will be decked out in their full dress finery.

Go also to the garden squares, the commons and the heaths of the suburbs. There, the long shadows cast by the early-morning sun create dramatic effects that are soon lost as the light intensifies and the sun rises higher in the sky.

Sunrise over the Thames

Go especially to the river. The Thames is at its most glorious at sunrise, as the first light strikes the buildings that line its banks. Stand on Westminster or Lambeth Bridge to watch the first rays catch the Houses of Parliament, or on Tower Bridge, a sight in itself, with the Tower of London close by. Or go to Island Gardens on the Isle of Dogs to see the view of Greenwich Palace immortalized by Canaletto. Further upstream, see the monolithic, now powerless, Battersea Power Station, its chimneys emerging from the early-morning mist like the legs of an upturned table. Designed by Sir Giles Gilbert Scott, Battersea Power Station has been empty since 1983. The latest in a long series of aborted plans for the derelict building is to turn it into a multi-screen cinema, two hotels, two theatres and a shopping complex. The cost will be £500 million and the façade of the building will be preserved. It remains to be seen whether this plan will meet with more success than others have done. In the meantime, the building continues to deteriorate, its only occasional use being as a dramatic background to films or photo shoots.

Wordsworth wrote of the view from Westminster Bridge: 'Earth has not anything to show more fair; /Dull would he be of soul who could pass by/A sight so touching in its majesty…' It is still lovely to stand on Westminster Bridge, but today the best view of all is to be had from Waterloo Bridge. The 'skyscapes' to the left and right are magnificent: facing the north bank, Big Ben, Westminster Abbey, Whitehall Court, Charing Cross

Battersea Power Station at dawn. When it was originally built in 1933, Battersea Power Station only had two chimneys. It was doubled in size in 1948 creating the outline for which it is famous. It fell into disrepair when it ceased functioning in 1983.

RIGHT The sun illuminates one of the many new buildings in the ancient City of London. Behind it is a tower that was, for many years, the tallest in the whole of London. It has now lost that distinction to Canary Wharf Tower, shown in the picture below. The pink coloured building on the right is Minster Court, which looks for all the world like a fairy castle.

BELOW RIGHT The great tower at Canary Wharf was the building that ensured the success on a massive scale of the Docklands redevelopment. Designed by Cesar Pelli and covered in stainless steel, it is by far the tallest building in Britain and can be seen from many miles away. Always dramatic, it is at its most stunning at dawn or dusk.

FAR RIGHT As the sun rises, cranes are silhouetted against an angry sky: proof positive of the colossal amount of building currently underway in the the City of London.

Station; Cleopatra's Needle to the west and, to the east, the dome of St Paul's, the spire of St Bride, the figure of Justice capping the Old Bailey and the triple towers of the Barbican.

Before Britain split from the continent 10,000 years ago, the Thames was a tributary of the mighty Rhine and, as great rivers of the world go, it is fairly insignificant in size. At only 346 kilometres (215 miles) long, it is by any account an undramatic, meandering river, but few others have been as important to a nation and its history. 2,000 years ago the Thames was bridged by the Romans, facilitating the establishment of one of the greatest cities in the world. The river became a conduit for trade and invasion and its strategic importance was recognized by each successive conqueror, who built fortifications along its banks. Remnants of such fortifications, dating from Roman and especially from Norman times, are still to be found in London: the massive Tower of London on the banks of the river, the best-known survivor, still

looks as impressive now as it did when it was first built nearly 1,000 years ago.

London became a port in Roman times, and by the 19th century was the biggest in the world. Now the Port of London, although still of world importance, is no longer to be found in the capital but has moved downstream to Tilbury, where the river is wide enough and deep enough to accommodate modern container vessels. London's old dock area has been transformed into a gleaming new city.

The Storm Water Pumping Station is one of the most interesting architectural delights of the newly developed Isle of Dogs, in Docklands. It was designed by John Outram and his brief specified that it must last for 100 years. Its purpose is to house the controls and maintenance for electric pumps below the floor, but the design of the building is 'derived from the idea that it should imitate a river and a landscape from which the storm-water flowed'. Thus the central section of the front wall is made of blue bricks, to imitate the river that flows between tree trunks, represented by the big round red central columns. The walls are stratified like the sides of a mountain, and the round hole of the ventilating fan that splits the

LEFT The Government has been much criticized for the amount of money spent on the Millennium Dome and, at the time of writing, the jury has yet to give its verdict on the success of the project. Everyone is agreed, though, that the structure, designed by Sir Richard Rogers, is full of drama.

ABOVE The architectural style of the Storm Water Pumping Station on the Isle of Dogs has been described as 'Post-Modern Egyptian Monumental'! The roundel in the pediment is not purely decorative but contains the fan which extracts methane gas from the building.

TOP The Thames Barrier at dawn. Protecting London from all danger of flooding, the barrier has been termed one of the wonders of the modern world.

New housing along the river at Chiswick. Despite these modern buildings, Chiswick still retains the atmosphere of the village it once was. Its proximity to the river makes it as desirable an address now, as it was for William Hogarth, Lord Burlington and William Morris in previous centuries.

gable into two triangular 'peaks' contains the source of the river, as if within a cave between the mountains. The sense of flood water is suggested by the building's proportions, which give the impression that, though the building is partly sub-merged, it is rising from the water.

The Thames has also been the setting for pageantry and festivities down the ages. Proces-sions of gaily caparisoned barges have carried roy-alty and the court up and down the river to the palaces that lined its banks, their passage often marked by music drifting across the water (Handel's Water Music was composed for a proces-sion on the Thames). The approach of kings or queens was heralded by fanfares of trumpets ring-ing across the water.

In the 17th and 18th centuries and the early years of the 19th century, the river would freeze over in cold winters and, upstream of old London Bridge, a fair was held on the ice. Stalls selling all manner of merchandise were set up, bears performed their tricks, fairground entertainments drew crowds to the river and whole oxen were roasted on the ice. The last Frost Fair was held in 1814. The old London Bridge had acted as a kind of dam, creating an area of still water upstream of its piers; when the bridge was removed and, later in the 19th century, the river was deepened and narrowed by embankments, the chances of the fast-flowing tidal river freezing were gone for ever.

The Thames was once at the heart of an active shipping industry, its banks lined with warehouses and cranes. The river was a busy thoroughfare, crammed with every type of vessel going up- or downstream, or weaving a passage across from bank to bank. In the congested area between London Bridge and Tower Bridge, a man could cross from bank to bank by clambering across the

ABOVE RIGHT Way to the
west, in Putney, sportsmen are
out exercising on the empty
stretches of the Thames.
On this side of London there
are many boat-houses along
the river, and some of the
local schools have strong
rowing traditions.

serried ranks of moored ships, barges and lighters waiting to load or unload their cargoes. Now that traffic has gone. The warehouses and cranes have largely disappeared and the river is no longer the commercial highway it once was, but in the early morning, before the remaining commercial traffic begins to crowd the river, scullers can be seen skimming along. The occasional barge laden with scrap can sometimes be seen chugging past Big Ben, and increasing numbers of pleasure craft ply their trade, showing off London from the river. Efforts are also being made to make more use of the river for public transport. While in the past many services have been started, only to close shortly afterwards, new piers have now been built and there seems to be a greater commitment on the part of the government to make these ventures successful. In the past the cost has proved prohibitive. It

remains to be seen whether this time any of these enterprises will prove viable and make the Thames the busy waterway it once was.

Now that great stretches of the river's banks are open and more people are able to walk along the river, some of the pageantry is returning. This was demonstrated by the spectacular river firework display on 31 December 1999, watched from the banks and bridges of the Thames by an estimated 4 million spectators. Water festivals and boat races are becoming increasingly popular. In March, in the week before their famous boat race, the Olympian figures of the Oxford and Cambridge crews might be seen practising in the early morning. Birds, too, are to be found in great numbers all along the river at first light, and the sight of a cormorant perched like a heraldic beast on a half-submerged post is no longer a rarity, even in the heart of London.

fort, a house for its governor and a surrounding defensive wall, fragments of which still survive. Since the 1980s extensive rebuilding has been carried out in the City and archaeologists, allowed onto sites before rebuilding begins, have uncovered much of Roman London that was previously unknown.

After the Romans left Britain in AD410, London all but crumbled until the Saxons began to redevelop it, using the fine Roman roads as foundations for their houses. A natural magnet for the predatory Norsemen, London was taken by the Vikings in the 9th century but later freed by Alfred the Great. Having gained control, Alfred fortified the City, rebuilding its walls to withstand further invasion. From then on, London grew

from strength to strength. So powerful was the City of London when William the Conqueror invaded in 1066 that he did not attempt to take it by force but instead negotiated a settlement with the burghers, issuing them with a charter that ratified their existing rights and privileges. The charter is still in existence.

All the rights and privileges of the City were established in the Middle Ages and have been jealously guarded ever since. The area has been self-governing since 1214 and has its own police force. The Corporation of the City of London acts through the Court of Common Council, which is presided over by the Lord Mayor, who is elected to office annually. The Court of Common Council is made up of 24 Aldermen, who hold office

RIGHT With the increase
of interest in the Isle of Dogs
from businesses, the City has
had to compete in order to
remain pre-eminent.
The result, over the last few
years, has been more and
more elegant, high tech
blocks, offering all the best
in modern amenities.

LEFT AND ABOVE A contrast within the City: the picture on the left shows a view from the south, as workers pour over London Bridge *en route* to their offices. Most are heading north, having arrived at London Bridge Station on the south bank. In recent years, the business community has extended into the district of Southwark, so some of the people are heading in the opposite direction. At the west end of the City, seen in the picture above, all is still peaceful around St Paul's. A worker goes about his business as the sun shines low across one of the few open spaces within the City.

for life, and 134 Common Councilmen elected annually by the ratepayers.

London has long been a cosmopolitan city, its narrow streets crowded by merchants from all over Europe since the earliest days. The Hanseatic League, the trading 'multinational' of its time, based in Hamburg and Lubeck, had a depot here until it was sent packing by Elizabeth I. The great Livery Companies (named for the dress or 'livery' that each adopted) were founded by the craftsmen of the medieval city to regulate trade and maintain standards. Still in existence today, the Livery Companies founded schools, some of which are considered among the country's finest, and built almshouses for the poor and the elderly.sure for more than a few years.

London's Financial Heart

RIGHT High in the pediment
of the Bank of England sits the
'Old Lady of Threadneedle
Street'. She carries a model
of the bank and is believed to
represent Britannia. This
sculpture plus the six butress
figures below representing
'bearers and guardians of
wealth', are the work of
Charles Wheeler and date
from the 1920s when the
bank was rebuilt.

The City has suffered many setbacks over the years but has always recovered. Rebuilt after the Great Fire of 1666 and again after the bombing of the Second World War, it remains one of the most important financial centres in the world. The chief offices of the principal banks, insurance companies, stockbrokers and mercantile houses are nearly all to be found within the 'Square Mile'. At the heart of the City stands Bank, the Piccadilly Circus of the Square Mile. On its north side, covering about 1.2 hectares (3 acres), is the great

ABOVE Grand buildings
at Bank. To the left, on
Threadneedle Street, is the
Bank of England, with
the Stock Exchange in the
distance. To the right is the
Royal Exchange, with one
of London's many statues of
the Duke of Wellington in
the foreground. The duke,
one of the country's greatest
commanders, was the victor
of the Battle of Waterloo,
which marked the end of
Britain's wars with France.

prison-like edifice of the Bank of England. It is familiarly known as the 'Old Lady of Threadneedle Street' and the old lady herself can be seen in the pediment overlooking the street. The Bank of England is the nation's bank, managing the national debt, fixing the interest rates of the country and issuing bank notes. Despite its name, it was privately owned until 1946, when it was nationalized. Founded in 1694 by the Scotsman William Patterson, it was established as a national bank for lending money to the government. With the promise of high interest rates the public subscribed enthusiastically and £1.2m was raised in just 11 days. The bank moved to its first purpose-built home in 1734. This building was replaced by a second building, designed by Sir John Soane, after riots in 1780 had raised a general awareness about

A fine view of the City from the river, showing its ancient and its modern face. To the left are modern office blocks. Note, particularly, how little that is old survives along the river. This was a target area during the Second World War, and has been almost entirely rebuilt since then. Happily, the ancient Tower of London, on the right, survived wartime bombs with minimal damage.

security – hence its windowless, forbidding appearance. Also as a result of the riots a detachment of the Brigade of Guards was sent to guard the bank, a practice that continued until 1973. The curtain wall is all that remains of Sir John Soane's building. Behind the wall stands the present building, dating from 1925, which has seven storeys above ground and three below. A small section of the bank is given over to a museum that tells its history and explains its function today. In the museum can be seen two gold ingots, the only gold that the bank itself owns. The huge stacks of ingots in its vaults belong to its customers.

The Royal Exchange on the east side of Bank is surmounted by a golden grasshopper, the emblem of the Gresham family, who built the first exchange in the 16th century. Richard Gresham had been inspired by the Bourse in Amsterdam and felt that London merchants should have their own trading centre, instead of doing business in the street or in the nave of St Paul's. Despite sup-

port from Henry VIII, the original scheme came to nought, and it was Thomas Gresham, Richard's son, who finally realized his father's dream. In January 1570, Elizabeth I dined with Sir Thomas, toured the building and caused it 'by an herald and trumpet to be proclaimed The Royal Exchange, and so to be called from henceforth and not otherwise'. This first exchange was destroyed by the Great Fire of 1666, to be replaced by another, which was also destroyed by fire in 1838. The present Royal Exchange was opened by Queen Victoria who, following the example of her predecessor, announced 'It is my royal will and pleasure that this building be hereafter called The Royal Exchange.' The steps outside, close to the equestrian statue of the Duke of Wellington, are one of the places in London from which a new monarch is proclaimed.

The Royal Exchange ceased to function in 1939, but the premises were used as a trading floor by LIFFE for some years afterwards. Today the building is used as offices, but its interior,

containing a Turkish pavement from the original exchange and paintings by Lord Leighton, Queen Victoria's favourite artist, can be seen by special arrangement.

Home of the Lord Mayor

Mansion House is the official residence of the Lord Mayor of London. Although there had been talk of giving the Mayor an official home for over a century, it was not until 1739 that the first foundation stone was laid. Within this stone (its position now forgotten) were placed coins, from a farthing to a guinea, minted in 1739. The architect was George Dance and his Palladian design had two curious additions that looked rather like large tombs sitting on the roof. Dubbed the 'Mayor's Nest' and 'Noah's Ark', these were later removed.

Within Mansion House is a courtroom (the Lord Mayor is the Chief Magistrate of the City) and 10 prison cells for men and one, 'the bird-cage', for women. Emmeline Pankhurst, one of the leading suffragettes, was once imprisoned here. Although Mansion House is only occasionally open to the public, a tantalizing glimpse of the magnificent interior, with its moulded ceilings, can be seen from the outside when the chandeliers are ablaze at night.

Lloyd's of London

Just beyond Bank, in Leadenhall Street, is Lloyd's of London. Designed by Sir Richard Rogers, the controversial building is either loved or loathed – it is impossible to be indifferent to it. Rogers reversed the normal office construction by placing all the services – lifts, staircases and lavatories – in six steel towers on the exterior of the building. This enabled him to create a vast 12-storey atrium in the centre of the building, with each floor linked by an escalator that zigzags up through the building. The extreme modernity of the design is all the more remarkable when one

RIGHT The entrance archway to the old Lloyd's of London building. Dating from the 1920s, the building reflects the type of grand design favoured when the British Empire was at its most powerful.

FAR RIGHT Lloyd's of London, with the International Financial Centre towering behind it. Whatever people may feel about modern architecture, Sir Richard Rogers' use of materials such as steel and glass ensures breathtaking reflections at sunrise.

considers that it was commissioned by such a very conservative institution.

Lloyd's began life in the 1680s in a City coffee house owned by Edward Lloyd. Here, ships' captains, merchants and shipowners gathered and the coffee house came to be known as a place where reliable news of shipping could be gathered and insurance for shipping be obtained. By 1771 the merchants had formed themselves into a committee and in 1774 took rooms in the Royal Exchange. Lloyd's, which was incorporated in 1811, remained in the Royal Exchange until 1928, when its first headquarters on the present site were built. Of the exterior of this original building only the entrance archway survives, sitting rather oddly alongside the modern steel structure. The Lutine bell, salvaged from the ship of that name, which sank in 1799, was placed in the centre of the present building. It used to be rung whenever there was a loss at sea. Now it can only be heard on ceremonial occasions, when it sounds twice for good news and once for bad.

Until 1993, Lloyd's accepted no corporate

liability for losses. It was made up of 'names' –
wealthy individual underwriters who covered
losses and took profits. The underwriters were
liable to the full extent of their private fortunes
to meet their insurance commitments. A succession of disasters threatened many of them with
bankruptcy and since 1993 Lloyd's has been
obliged to limit the liability of its 'names'.
Although originally only shipping was insured at
Lloyd's it has, since 1911, insured anything,
though it does not provide long-term life assur-
ance. The legs of Hollywood star Betty Grable are
a fabled example.

ABOVE AND RIGHT Early sun reflected in
the steel exterior of the Lloyd's building is
in turn reflected in the glass of the tower
in the background. It would be interesting
to know what the City's greatest architect,
Sir Christopher Wren, would have
thought of some of its present buildings.
In his day, Wren was pushing technology
to the limit and experimenting with every
building he designed. The church on the
right, St Stephen Walbrook, is a typical
example of his pioneering work.

A Wren Masterpiece

The Church of St Stephen Walbrook, like so many buildings in the City, has a long history. The delightful Wren church seen today stands on what was once a little stream, the Walbrook, a long-vanished tributary of the River Thames. The original church was founded before 1096; its successor of 1429 was destroyed in the Great Fire of 1666 and rebuilt by Sir Christopher Wren in the 1670s. The church provided Wren with a testing ground for some of the theories he would later put into practice in St Paul's Cathedral. A book reviewing the buildings of London, published in 1732, praised St Stephen Walbrook, describing it as 'famous all over Europe and justly reputed the masterpiece of the celebrated Sir Christopher. Perhaps Italy itself can produce no modern buildings that can vie with this in taste or proportion.' Despite the fact that the church suffered severe bomb damage in 1940, much of its fine 17th-century interior work has survived to bear testimony to the skill of Wren and his craftsmen. Sir John Vanbrugh, playwright and architect, is buried in the vault.

Since the 1950s the church has been famous as the first home of the Samaritans, an organization that seeks to help those who are unhappy and may be contemplating suicide. The organisation was founded by the then Rector of St Stephen, Dr Chad Varah. The Samaritans themselves are dedicated volunteers who, after rigorous training, staff telephones throughout the day and night, speaking for as long as is needed – sometimes hours at a time – to callers in emotional distress. It is impossible to quantify the amount of hope these unpaid volunteers have given, or the number of lives they have saved.

The church underwent an extensive restoration when one of its more controversial elements was installed: the round stone altar, commissioned from the modern English sculptor Henry Moore, which was immediately and irreverently nicknamed 'the Camembert'. This restoration was completed in 1987.

'The car, the furniture, the wife, the children –
everything is disposable. Because you see the
main thing today is – shopping.'

ARTHUR MILLER

Opening-time in the

West End

The 'West End' is an area with no clearly defined boundaries. Everyone knows what is meant by the term, but to say exactly where it starts and stops is difficult. It certainly includes the shops of Oxford Street, Regent Street, Piccadilly and Bond Street, along with the theatre district of Piccadilly Circus (the Times Square of London), Leicester Square, Covent Garden and Shaftesbury Avenue. The West End means, to most people, the wealthy squares and streets of Mayfair, the shops – from huge department stores to small boutiques – the theatres, cinemas and restaurants that come alive later in the day. It spells glamour and excitement as much to suburban Londoners as to London's visitors. Going 'up West' to Eastenders means having an exciting time.

Except for a few isolated clusters of buildings, the area west of the City of London – the area we think of today as the West End – was countryside until after the Great Fire of London in 1666. Then, many wealthier citizens chose not to rebuild within the old city, but to move west instead. At the time, Charles II had recently been restored to the throne and the Court of St James's re-established. The area surrounding St James's Palace, home of the monarch, became immensely fashionable – *the* place to live.

The First Squares

The latter part of the 17th century saw the emergence of a new type of development west of the City: the birth of the 'London square'. Instead of the narrow, twisting streets of the City, roads were wide and straight and led to and from squares. The first such square was laid out by the 4th Earl of Southampton on his land at Bloomsbury. He built a grand house for himself on one side of the square and let the other sides in even-sized plots at rents

Bedford Square is the finest of the Bloomsbury squares and survives quite unspoiled. When it was first built in 1775, the streets approaching it were gated, reserved for the exclusive use of residents. The owners of the surrounding houses still have sole use of the central oval garden, although Bedford Square is no longer residential and all the houses are now offices.

ABOVE Bedford Square was conceived as four palace fronts facing one another across a garden. This is why the central houses on each side, pictured here, look grander than the others and their brick exteriors are clad in decorative stucco.

RIGHT Coade stone, from which this ornament was made, was used extensively in 18th-century London. Artificially made, it was extremely weatherproof, and many well-known sculptors worked with the material.

reasonable enough to ensure that speculators built on them. The leases were for 42 years, at the end of which time ownership reverted to the Southamptons, who were then able to re-let them for their own profit. Southampton (now Blooms-bury Square) was like a little town, with side streets, carriage mews and a market for local inhabitants. The next square to be built, St James's, even boasted its own church – St James in Pic-cadilly. This famous thoroughfare forms the southern boundary of Mayfair, the smartest – and most expensive – part of central London. There was a 'May fair' there once, which centred on Shepherd Market, but it was suppressed as a public nuisance: 'I never in my life saw such a

ABOVE AND RIGHT Trees and statuary in Berkeley Square. The square was laid out in the 1730s and 40s, but has since been much rebuilt, and the London plane trees in the garden were planted around 1790. Berkeley Square was originally one of the most aristocratic squares in London, with many famous residents, of whom Lord Clive of India is perhaps the best remembered today.

number of lazy-looking rascals and so hateful a throng of beggarly, sluttish strumpets', said an observer. Wealth and something approaching decorum now characterize Mayfair's handsome squares, Grosvenor and Berkeley, although the murmurings of croupiers are occasionally to be heard behind a façade.

Open for Business

The West End's day begins a little later than that of the City. It is not until close to 9am that the shop assistants hurry from crowded Tubes and buses to ready their shops and department stores for customers. Theirs will be a day spent

LEFT Harrods Meat Hall is one of the most spectacular sights in any shop in London. Dating from 1901, the interior is decorated with tiled pictures of hunting scenes and peacocks, and the tiles are 'listed' to ensure that they cannot be removed. Each day, before the store opens, great love and care are lavished on creating a perfect display of meat. So dazzling is the result that it seems a shame to disturb it by making a purchase!

Harrods was first established in 1849 as a small grocer's shop. It expanded steadily until 1883, when the shop was destroyed by fire just before Christmas. Mr Harrod sent out a letter saying that because of the fire orders might be 'delayed in the execution a day or two'. He managed to send all the orders in time for Christmas and this so impressed his customers that by the time the store was rebuilt in 1884 his turnover had doubled. The first moving staircase in London was installed in Harrods in 1898 (smelling-salts and brandy were offered at the top to nervous customers!) and the famous frontage in terracotta brickwork dates from 1901.

LEFT Harrods Meat Hall is one of the most spectacular sights in any shop in London. Dating from 1901, the interior is decorated with tiled pictures of hunting scenes and peacocks, and the tiles are 'listed' to ensure that they cannot be removed. Each day, before the store opens, great love and care are lavished on creating a perfect display of meat. So dazzling is the result that it seems a shame to disturb it by making a purchase!

Harrods was first established in 1849 as a small grocer's shop. It expanded steadily until 1883, when the shop was destroyed by fire just before Christmas. Mr Harrod sent out a letter saying that because of the fire orders might be 'delayed in the execution a day or two'. He managed to send all the orders in time for Christmas and this so impressed his customers that by the time the store was rebuilt in 1884 his turnover had doubled. The first moving staircase in London was installed in Harrods in 1898 (smelling-salts and brandy were offered at the top to nervous customers!) and the famous frontage in terracotta brickwork dates from 1901.

RIGHT The art deco barber's shop at Austin Reed is one of the great secrets of Regent Street. Preserving the original basins and chairs, the chevron screens in chrome and frosted glass, and the eye-catching wave-scroll ceiling light, this interior is the most complete of its kind in London.

BELOW It is no surprise that the old, established cheese shop of Paxton and Whitfield stands in Jermyn Street, one of the finest, if most expensive, old shopping streets of London. The shop was originally founded by a Suffolk cheesemonger at Clare Market in about 1740. Today, every imaginable cheese, from all over the world, is to be found here.

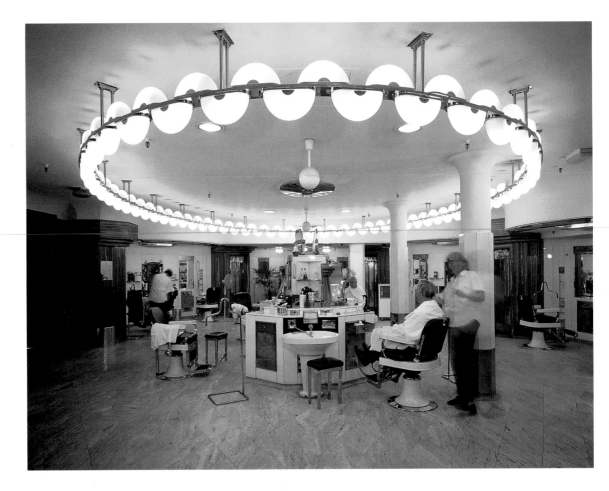

indoors in artificial light. Many avail themselves of the opportunity to take in some fresh air on their way to work by cutting across the central London parks or squares. At this time in the morning, the great expanses of grass are empty, except for grazing pigeons and stacked deck-chairs, but the concrete paths that cross the open areas become streams of hurrying workers on their way to work.

Inside the shops a brief period of near-frantic activity is followed by a few moments of calm. The shelves are stacked, everything is in order and the staff wait fresh and alert for the doors to open. In the famous food halls at Harrods, the day's displays have been artistically arranged. The art-deco barber's shop in Austin Reed awaits its first clients. At Paxton and Whitfield in Jermyn Street the cheeses are piled high and the smell is intoxicating. The aroma of well-waxed leather will greet the horseman who steps into Swaine, Adeney, Brigg and Sons to buy his saddle or bridle. In Lib-

erty in Regent Street the carpets are draped over the wooden railings to hang suspended above several floors, as if in some exotic eastern bazaar. In Hamleys all is peaceful before bright-eyed children descend on the store with parents muttering about 'the cost of things these days'.

A Shopper's Paradise

It is possible to buy anything in London – from left-handed scissors to ship's compasses, from china to guns, from poisonous snakes to flowers. Some streets specialize in certain goods: Oxford Street has shoe shops aplenty, in Regent Street shops selling china or glass stand cheek by jowl with film-company stores like Disney and Warner Bros. Piccadilly has an assortment of shops, though when the street was first developed, almost every shop was a bookshop. Hatchard's, which dates from the 18th century, is the sole survivor. Tottenham Court Road was once famous for its furniture stores, but these have now mostly disappeared, and it is computers, hi-fi and electrical equipment

ABOVE John Hatchard opened his bookshop in 1797 at No. 173 Piccadilly, moving to its current premises, further along the road, in 1801. It became a fashionable rendezvous, with the atmosphere of a club rather than a shop. Daily newspapers were laid out on the table by the fire and benches were supplied outside for the customers' servants. Behind the shop was a reading room, where the inaugural meeting of the Royal Horticultural Society was held. The room was also used by William Wilberforce for anti-slavery meetings.

RIGHT Piccadilly Arcade links Jermyn Street and Piccadilly, providing a delightful shopping mall.

CLOCKWISE FROM TOP LEFT This montage of famous shops features Fortnum & Mason in Piccadilly at top left. Mr Charles Fortnum was a footman to George III. One of the perks of the job was that he was allowed to sell the candles that had been used for only short times in the palace. With the proceeds, he teamed up with his friend John Mason and founded a store, close to the present site, in the 1770s. From the first, it was patronized by high society and royalty. The traditional Fortnum & Mason hampers were first prepared for visitors to the Great Exhibition of 1851.

James Smith & Sons (centre) have been supplying umbrellas and sticks from this famous shop in New Oxford Street since 1830.

Lock & Co. in St James's Street (top right) was established here in 1764. Customers included Lord Nelson, who had a hat with a built-in eyeshade specially made, and the Duke of Wellington, who bought the plumed hat that he wore at the battle of Waterloo in 1815. It was Locks who invented the 'bowler hat', originally called a 'coke', after William Coke, who asked for a hard hat that could be worn by his gamekeepers when chasing poachers.

Nothing can be more enticing on a winter's day than the sparkling interior of Mrs Crick's Chandelier shop in Kensington High Street (bottom right).

Burlington Arcade, (bottom centre) built in 1818, is lined with mahogany-fronted shops selling mainly antiques and traditional fashions. Today it is still patrolled, as it has been from the start, by its own security force of frock-coated Beadles, who ensure that no one runs, sings or engages in 'unseemly behaviour'.

The Queen of Time presides over the main entrance to Selfridges (bottom left). This huge department store was opened by Gordon Selfridge in 1909. He was from Chicago, where he had become a junior partner at Marshal Field. He had bought his own store in Chicago but was unhappy setting up in competition with the shop that had trained him. He sold up and moved to Europe, eventually building this store in Oxford Street as a rival to Harrods.

Floris of Jermyn Street (middle left) was established by a Spanish barber from Minorca in 1730. For his fashionable clientele he began concocting perfumes reminiscent of the fragrant flowers of his home. Soon they became so successful that he stopped cutting hair and concentrated solely on perfume. The Spanish mahogany display cases inside were acquired from the Great Exhibition of 1851.

Covent Garden, on the eastern verge of the West End, does not come to life until about 11am. The shops are open seven days a week, usually from 10am to 7pm. There are many small boutiques selling clothes, jewellery and craft goods. One of Britain's most popular chocolate shops, Thorntons, is also to be found here.

that draw the consumers. This is about the only street in London where the shopper is positively encouraged to haggle, as each shop vies with its neighbours to provide the lowest price.

In January and July – the traditional sales times in London – the calm before opening time is particularly welcomed by the staff, who know they will be in for a day of scrambling and pushing and of frenetic selling as swarms of eager shoppers fight over the best bargains. Christmas, too, is hard work: the rush begins the moment the doors open and the shops stay open for many additional hours. But that is only for a few exhausting weeks

of the year. Most of the time the first hour or so of trading will be relatively quiet and the staff can slip gently into the day's routine.

Those who work in the grand shops catering for the wealthy may have it particularly easy, as these luxurious emporiums will usually not open their doors until 10am or later. In Saville Row or Jermyn Street, where the gentleman of leisure has traditionally purchased his handmade suit or shirt, the tailors will not expect their customers for several hours yet. But this is exceptional – by 9 or 9.30am most of the West End retail outlets are open.

As the shop doors open, the great tourist sights

are also preparing for the onslaught of visitors. By 11.30 the West End – indeed the whole of London – is vibrant with life.

Heart of the West End

Trafalgar Square is one of the West End's most popular attractions. People go there to have fun – to feed the pigeons, paddle in the fountains, clamber over the lions. At Christmas they go there to admire the huge Christmas tree (an annual gift from the people of Norway) and sing carols at its foot, and at New Year they converge on the square from all directions in the hope of hearing Big Ben strike midnight. After important football matches at Wembley Stadium, Trafalgar Square is the chosen place of celebration for the fans of the victorious side.

Trafalgar Square is also a 'protest' square. Almost as soon as it was laid out, it was recognized as a suitable open space in which to start or finish demonstrations. The Chartists were the first to use it for such purposes, in 1848, and in the 1960s it was the focus of the CND protests. Today there are regular gatherings here of every imaginable form of pressure group.

One of London's grandest open spaces, Trafalgar Square was laid out between 1829 and 1841, and named after the Battle of Trafalgar, the famous victory at sea over the French in 1805. The hero of the hour and commander of the English fleet, who

The neoclassical central market building of Covent Garden was completed in 1830, and the iron and glass roof was added between 1875 and 1889. When the fruit and vegetable market moved out, the whole area might have fallen victim to redevelopment (one of the plans was for a dual carriageway through the square), and this fine building might have vanished. Happily, it was saved and splendidly restored, reopening in its present form in 1980.

LEFT Trafalgar Square is filling with people and pigeons, and will remain crowded all day. The fountains spring to life at 10 am each morning, causing all the birds momentarily to take flight. The basins and fountains in their present form date from1939; the basins are lined with blue to give light and colour to the water.

ABOVE RIGHT The bronze dolphins, mermaids and mermen of the Trafalgar Square fountains were added after the Second World War. The fine spray of water that constantly falls on the bronze helps to maintain its gleaming patina.

BELOW RIGHT In the mid-19th century the water was supplied to the fountains from two wells – one in front of the National Gallery and one behind it. The wells were connected by a tunnel that passed under the gallery. This water supply eventually dried up and was replaced by a town mains. Now the powerful water jets are driven by electric pumps.

died during the battle, was Horatio Nelson. It is his statue, atop its 51 metre (167 foot) column, that dominates the square. 'The Nelson Monument' is its official name, but everyone calls it Nelson's Column. At its foot are the four bronze, guardian lions by Sir Edward Landseer, cast from cannon recovered from a ship that sank off Spithead in 1782, with 'twice 400 men' on board. The reliefs at the base of the column were also cast from cannon captured from the French. They show scenes from Nelson's battles – St Vincent, the Nile, Copenhagen and, of course, Trafalgar.

Nelson's Column was the site of a coup by Greenpeace a few years ago, when some athletic members climbed up the column very early one morning. By the time London woke up, they had unfurled an enormous banner. The police made no attempt to reach the protesters, who stayed triumphantly atop the column for some hours before finally negotiating a descent. Climbing the column is no small feat, so it is left to a steeplejack to clean it of pigeon droppings every other year.

RIGHT The National Gallery stretches across the north side of Trafalgar Square. The oldest part of the building is the central portico, which incorporates columns from the magnificent Carlton House demolished when George IV ascended the throne in 1820. Carlton House had been his home when he was Prince Regent, but on his accession he decided he needed something even grander.

FAR RIGHT A view across Trafalgar Square to St- Martin-in-the-Fields. The design for this church has been copied all over the world. There are versions of St Martin's in places as far apart as the United States and India.

Noble Neighbours

Three sides of Trafalgar Square are flanked by impressive buildings. To the north stands the National Gallery, one of the most important galleries in the world. It houses the nation's collection of European paintings dating from the 13th to the 19th century. It is not a big collection, by world standards, but has exceptionally fine paintings from every school of European art.

The gallery was founded in 1824, when the government of the day purchased just 38 paintings from the collection of an émigré financier, John Julius Angerstein, who had died the previous year. Unlike most of the great national collections of Europe, it was not based on royal collection, but has been built up by purchases over the years. Virtually all of its 2,050 or so paintings are on display.

The National Gallery's present building was designed by William Wilkins, its first home having been in Pall Mall. Extensions have been made over the years to accommodate the growing collection, most notably the Sainsbury Wing. This was designed by the American architect Robert Venturi; the first design, by Richard Rogers, was described by the Prince of Wales as 'a monstrous carbuncle on the face of a much-loved and elegant friend'. Some people feel that the Sainsbury Wing is rather bland and that the exterior adds nothing to the architecture of Trafalgar Square, but the interior, where the earliest paintings in the collection are now displayed, is acknowledged by all as being a magnificent space.

St Martin-in-the-Fields, the lovely church by James Gibbs in the north-west corner of the square, may seem inappropriately named today, but the original church stood in the fields between the City of London and Westminster. The church was the first home of the Academy

A panoramic view of the east side of the square, showing South Africa House to the left, and the end of the Strand and Charing Cross in the centre. Behind the base of Nelson's Column, to the right, is the top of Whitehall.

of St Martin-in-the-Fields, the world-renowned chamber orchestra, and the musical tradition is still upheld today, with lunch-time and evening concerts. The church has always opened its doors to the homeless, and there are usually people sleeping peacefully and undisturbed in the pews. When they wake up, there is a soup kitchen in the crypt for their sustenance. Also in the crypt, the more affluent can enjoy a meal in the restaurant or try their hand at brass rubbing, before browsing in the open-air market in the churchyard above.

St Martin-in-the-Fields is the parish church of the Sovereign, as most of Buckingham Palace is within the parish. Indeed, King George I was the first churchwarden of the new church, the only monarch ever to have held such a post. Charles II was baptised in the earlier church on the site and his mistress, the actress Nell Gwynne, was buried there.

Flanking Trafalgar Square, to the west, is Canada House, the headquarters of the High Commission for Canada; on the east side stands South Africa House. This was an embassy until South Africa had its first democratic elections in 1994, after which the country was invited to rejoin the Commonwealth and the building became once more a High Commission. During its embassy days an ongoing vigil was maintained outside, protesting against the apartheid regime and demanding the release from prison of Nelson Mandela. Some Londoners, sympathetic to the cause and frequently passing through Trafalgar Square, signed the petition many times. So it was appropriate that Nelson Mandela was welcomed triumphantly to Trafalgar Square by cheering crowds when, on a visit to London in August 1996, he made a speech from the balcony of South Africa House.

Royal Connections

The open area to the south of Trafalgar Square, at the top of Whitehall, is Charing Cross. On a little traffic island stands a fine equestrian statue of King Charles I by Hubert le Sueur. When Charles was executed in 1649, a certain John Rivett, a brazier, was ordered to destroy the statue. He made a small fortune selling 'relics' of its metal to Royalist supporters. However, when King Charles II was restored to the throne, the statue was miraculously returned intact! It had spent the intervening years buried in Mr Rivett's garden. It was erected in its present position in 1675 and on 30 January each year, the anniversary of the death of Charles I, wreaths are placed on its pedestal by the Royal Stuart Society.

Long before the statue of the 'martyr king' was erected, an Eleanor Cross stood on roughly the same site. After the death of King Edward I's beloved wife Eleanor in 1291, the king himself gave orders that a cross was to be erected on each of the twelve sites at which the funeral cortège bringing her body to Westminster Abbey from Nottinghamshire had rested on its journey. The final cross was placed here, at the village of Charing. The original cross was removed in 1647 but there is a 19th-century replica in the forecourt of Charing Cross Station. Dr Johnson, the great 18th-century writer and lexicographer, said: 'Fleet Street has a very animated appearance, but I think the full tide of human existence is at Charing Cross.' It is appropriate, then, that this great hub of London is regarded as the centre of the metropolis, and a tablet in the ground close to the statue of Charles I is the point from which all distances to and from London are measured.

'Oh, London is a fine town,
A very famous city,
Where all the streets are paved with gold,
And all the maidens pretty.'

GEORGE COLMAN THE YOUNGER

Mid-morning Bustle

By mid-morning London is fully awake. The principal thoroughfares are crowded with buses, tourist coaches, taxis and delivery vans attempting to offload in streets not designed for the purpose. Messengers on motor bikes and bicycles thread their way through traffic, momentarily tailing back from the lights. At 11am each weekday bound packs of the first editions of the *Evening Standard*, London's only evening newspaper, are tossed from vans to waiting vendors – a process that is repeated throughout the day with each new edition.

If they are sensible, it is not until now, after the early-morning rush hour, that tourists venture into London's Underground, finding their way through an often labyrinthine series of tunnels and discovering that the system is not as incomprehensible as they had feared. Armed with their daily or weekly passes, they discover the mysteries of the barriers, the etiquette of the escalators and familiarize themselves with the meaning of 'Bakerloo', 'District', 'Northern', 'Victoria' and 'Jubilee'.

Some visitors will prefer to travel above ground. They may discover that all bus stops are not the same and that the bus they have waited for patiently may sweep past them if they are at a 'request' stop, and soon learn that an arm has to be extended to catch the eye of the driver. They will also learn that a £10 note will not be viewed with much favour by that same driver and that something closer to the right money is expected, to cover a fare on London's buses. By the end of their first day's travel on public transport, the visitors will have had some adventures, but will have mastered the system and feel, rightly, that they are beginning to understand how London works. The wealthier visitors emerging from the Ritz or the Savoy, from Claridges or the Dorchester, will be experiencing their first taxi rides and may be

What better way to approach the Tower of London than across Tower Bridge, built in Gothic style. The huge towers are constructed of stone- clad steel and support the great weight of the bascules. The original hydraulic lifting mechanism can today be seen in the museum within the bridge. Even though the Thames is not as busy as it once was, the central section of the bridge is raised a number of times each week to allow tall ships to pass through.

savouring or enduring the anecdotes of one of
the more loquacious drivers.

By mid-morning the shops are busy, and many
people already laden with packages will seek a
coffee and a Danish pastry before rejoining the
crowded pavements. The galleries and museums
too, are filling up. The noise level in the British
Museum, for example, slowly rises, as more and
more school parties flood in to study the Romans
in Britain, the Egyptian mummies or the wonders
of Ancient Greece.

National Treasures

The British Museum is one of the great trea-
sure houses of the world and is visited by
some six million people each year. It opened in
1759 and was the first national museum in the
world. The founder of the collection was Sir Hans
Sloane, who owned much of Chelsea, where many
streets still bear his name. He made provision in his
will for the nation to buy his vast collection for a
mere £20,000. It was worth at least four times as

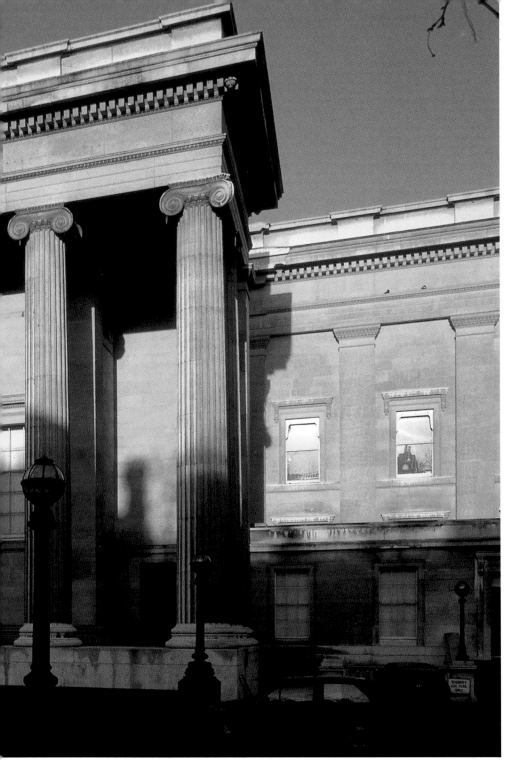

being made will allow greater access to the museum's astonishing collection of antiquities. The Great Court, which contained the British Library's famous circular Reading Room, has undergone substantial change now that the library has moved to new 'high-tech' premises at St Pancras.

Among the many exhibits to be seen at the museum are the Elgin Marbles. These sculptures once adorned the largest of the temples on the Acropolis, the Parthenon, in Athens, and were brought to England by Lord Elgin in 1802. They had been sold to Lord Elgin by the Turks, who at that time occupied Greece. Understandably, the Greeks now want them back. There is also a magnificent collection of Egyptian mummies, now in

FAR RIGHT The east wing of the British Museum, where the British Library was housed until its move in 1998 to St Pancras.

much, but as the government of the day was not prepared to pay, the money was raised by public lottery. Enough was raised to buy Sloane's Collection, several other collections and a mansion, Montague House, to put them in. Today's British Museum stands on the same site, having gradually absorbed the original building.

The present building dates from the 19th century: the monumental façade and its imposing portico was completed in 1851. Work on the interior of the museum continues today. The changes

new galleries, a fine collection of Chinese and Indian art, sculptures and reliefs from Assyria and, in the British section, the Lindow Man and the Sutton Hoo Ship Burial, which led historians to a much greater understanding of the 'Dark Ages'. If you want to see one of the seven wonders of the ancient world – the Mausoleum at Halicarnassus – it is no good going to Turkey, where it originally stood: today, most of what remains of this gigantic tomb is also to be found in the British Museum.

LEFT The Grand Piazza of the British Library. The arresting statue of Sir Isaac Newton is the work of Eduardo Paolozzi. The British Library took many years to complete and the design has been the subject of some criticism. However, the majority of readers, are very happy with the facilities within.

RIGHT A wall of books within the British Library makes a dramatic sight. The British Library is a 'copyright library', and a copy of every book, magazine and newspaper printed in Britain has to be lodged with the library. Originally containing books given by King George III, the library now has over 15 million books. Apart from the reading areas, there are three fine exhibition rooms displaying some of the library's treasures, which include the Magna Carta and the Lindisfarne Gospel.

LEFT The Natural History
Museum is one of the most
attractive buildings in London.
It was designed by Alfred
Waterhouse and built
between 1873 and 1880.
Very popular with children,
the museum houses exhibits
on everything from a
dinosaur to a flea.

RIGHT The Tate Gallery
houses the greater part
of the national collection
of British paintings, including
a huge collection of the
work of Turner, the great
19th-century landscape
artist. The gallery takes
its name from Sir Henry Tate,
the sugar refiner, who
commissioned the building
and gave his own collection
of 65 paintings to the nation.

As is the case in all large museums, it can be confusing finding your way to the object you most want to see. If you have limited time, the best way to see the greatest pieces in the British Museum is to take a tour of the highlights. The highly trained guides (London's *Blue Badge* Guides) are excellent, and will make sure that in an hour or so you will emerge from the museum having been stimulated, entertained and informed.

Popular exhibitions – the Impressionists or Rembrandt, perhaps, or the Summer Exhibition at the Royal Academy – also always draw the crowds, and by mid-morning the queues will be already stretching around the block. The queues at regular tourist honey-pots, such as Madame Tussaud's, the famous waxworks at Baker Street, or the London Dungeon in Southwark will also be a daunting sight by this time, and many will decide to save their visit for another day, little realizing that there is no quiet time at these places.

Special Days, Special Attractions

LEFT A sunny day
at Speaker's Corner, and
a colourful speaker sounds
forth. Whatever the weather,
Speaker's Corner always
attracts the crowds.

ABOVE Paintings on the
north railings of Green Park,
at the west end of Piccadilly.
The better-known outdoor
art gallery is along the railings
of Hyde Park. However, in
recent years paintings have
invaded these Green Park
railings, where at one time
there were only souvenirs
and bargain leather goods
on offer. The Green Park
site functions throughout
the weekend.

On some days of the week London has special attractions. On Sunday mornings, for example, one of London's gentler demonstrations of the right to free speech can be enjoyed at Speaker's Corner in Hyde Park. Here, anyone who has anything to say on any subject can get up on a box and make a speech. Everyone else comes to listen and heckle; occasionally, a real orator will delight the crowds. The only provisos are that there must be no contravention of the Public Order Act and that Royal Park Regulations must be observed. Many of the speakers today are from other parts of the world and are exercising a freedom of speech they do not enjoy in their own countries.

After joining the crowds to witness 'Democracy in action' at Speaker's Corner, the visitor can walk along the edge of Hyde Park to enjoy what has been termed the 'longest picture gallery in the world'. A regular gathering of artists hang their paintings along a particular, licensed, section of the park's railings, and the public come to look, admire and sometimes to buy. So popular is this area among artists that the waiting-list for a pitch is long. Once an artist has been awarded a space, he or she will hold on to it, even after becoming established and holding exhibitions at professional galleries. Sometimes it is possible to pick up the work of an established artist at Hyde Park at a fraction of the cost that the same work would command in a gallery. There is a strong sense of community along the north railings in Hyde Park and The Swan, the attractive pub situated halfway along, does a roaring trade among artists and public alike.

A Rich Ceremonial Life

Mid-morning is the time for pageantry in London. The best-known and perhaps favourite of such events is the Changing of the Guard at Buckingham Palace, which takes place daily in summer and on alternate days in winter. It is performed, usually, by troops from the five Guards regiments – the Grenadiers, the Coldstream, the Scots, the Irish and the Welsh. Occasionally, when the Guard regiments are not available, the honour of guarding the palace is undertaken in their place by other regiments, such as the Gurkhas.

Although the ceremony is centred on Buckingham Palace, the troops also form a ceremonial guard at Clarence House, the Queen Mother's London home, and St James's Palace, the London home of the Prince of Wales. The scarlet dress jackets worn by the guards look at first sight to be identical, but those in the know can pick out which regiment is on duty by studying the plumes on their bearskins and the arrangement of buttons on their tunics.

It is difficult for tourists to imagine that these soldiers have any place in an army of today. However, a glance at their modern rifles gives a hint that these are real soldiers and that when they are

LEFT The base of the Queen Victoria Monument, with Queen Victoria herself facing down the Mall.
The present Mall, with the monument at one end and Admiralty Arch at the other, was laid out as a national memorial to Queen Victoria between 1903 and 1904.

RIGHT A Welsh Guard on duty outside St James's Palace. This rambling palace was built for Henry VIII as a hunting lodge, and was the official residence of the monarch in London from 1698 until Queen Victoria moved to Buckingham Palace. Today, St James's Palace is the London home of the Prince of Wales.

not on London duty, they are to be found serving with the rest of the army in conflicts and as peace-keeping forces around the world.

Just across St James's Park is Horse Guards Parade. Here, at 11 each morning (10am on Sundays), the Mounting of the Horse Guards can be seen. There are two Household Cavalry regiments – the Life Guards and the Blues and Royals – they change over each day. The really keen (and fit) tourist may manage to catch both the Changing of the Guard at Buckingham Palace and the Mounting of the Guard at Horse Guards Parade in the same morning. The foot soldiers at Buckingham Palace are on duty for two hours at a time, and are allowed to keep themselves alert by marching a few steps up and

down every so often – a luxury not afforded to the horses. The horses have to remain stationary, so their guard duty lasts for one hour. From time to time, the guard duty at Horse Guards is performed by the King's Troop, the Royal Horse Artillery also responsible for the gun salutes heard on ceremonial and state occasions in Hyde Park and elsewhere.

A Birthday Tradition

The Trooping of the Colour, one such ceremonial occasion, is held in June each year to mark the monarch's official birthday. It first took place in 1755 and has been a regular part of London's ceremonial life since 1805. Its origin lies

LEFT Mounting the Guard takes place at Horse Guards Parade, watched by the usual crowd of tourists. The line of troopers are from the Blues and Royals Regiment, which was created out of the amalgamation, in 1969, of two regiments originally formed in the 17th century. This regiment and the Life Guards are two of the seven regiments that together make up the Household Division. The reigning sovereign is always the Colonel-in-Chief of the Household Division.

RIGHT A trooper of the Life Guards, easily recognized by his scarlet tunic and white plumed helmet. The troopers of the Blues and Royals have dark tunics and red plumed helmets.

The Palace of Westminster with the Victoria Tower in the foreground showing the entrance taken by the monarch at the State Opening of Parliament. At the other end of the building, Big Ben can be seen rising in the background.

in the need for soldiers to be able to recognize the regimental standards – 'the colours' – of their particular battalion, around which they were expected to rally in battle. The colours were paraded up and down the troops, who were lined up to observe them. This still happens in this now traditional ceremony, although certainly not on a modern battlefield.

Trooping the Colour takes place on the second Saturday in June at Horse Guards Parade. Each year a different 'colour' is trooped. The monarch always takes the salute, traditionally on horseback. When she was younger, the Queen rode from Buckingham Palace, side-saddle, to the Trooping. However, since her favourite and most reliable charger, Burmese, was retired in 1986, she has arrived in a carriage and taken the salute from a specially constructed dais.

The Queen's Speech

The State Opening of Parliament takes place in late October or early November or, in the case of a new Parliament, shortly after a general election. The tradition dates back to the 16th century, although the ritual of the 'monarch's speech' – the climax of the ceremony – can be traced back to the 13th century. Like many of the great events in London, the procession can be enjoyed for nothing, although the major part of the event – the monarch's speech to the two Houses of Parliament – is not open to the public.

For the occasion, the Queen is driven from Buckingham Palace to the Palace of Westminster in the Irish State Coach, accompanied by the Sovereign's Escort of Household Cavalry. She is preceded by another carriage, empty except for the

PRECEDING PAGES The Palace
of Westminster houses the
supreme legislature of Great
Britain and Northern Ireland
and has two chambers – the
House of Commons and the
House of Lords. The present
building was designed by
Sir Charles Barry, with
Augustine Pugin assisting
with the details, especially
those of the interior, and was
opened by Queen Victoria
in 1852, although it was
not completed for another
30 years. The building covers
more than 3 hectares
(8 acres), has 11 courtyards,
100 staircases and over 1,000
apartments, but is not
adequate for present needs.
As a result, the surrounding
buildings have been taken
over for use as additional
office space for Members
of Parliament and their staff.

LEFT AND RIGHT Richard I
in Old Palace Yard. This fine
bronze equestrian statue dates
from 1861 and is the work of
Carlo Marochetti. Richard,
Coeur de Lion (the Lion
Heart', is remembered fondly
in England as one of the great
early warrior kings. He ruled
for just 10 years (1189–1199),
of which two were spent
imprisoned for ransom in
Austria. He was succeeded by
his brother, 'bad' King John.

LEFT The House of Lords. Following the destruction of the old Palace of Westminster by fire in 1834, architects were asked to submit plans for a new Parliament in the 'Gothic or Elizabethan style'. Ninety- seven designs were submitted and those of Sir Charles Barry were chosen. He was really more at home with classical structures, however, so he asked Augustine Pugin, a Gothic specialist, to help him. The result, as Pugin famously remarked, was 'All grecian, sir; Tudor details on a classic body'.

RIGHT The Victoria Tower at the west end of the Palace of Westminster houses the archives of Parliament. It contains over 3 million documents including all the Acts of Parliament since 1497. When completed in 1858, at 323 feet high it was the tallest square tower in the world.

Imperial State Crown, which travels in lonely splendour on a cushion. When the Queen reaches Westminster, her arrival is signalled by a salute of guns fired by the King's Troop of the Royal Horse Artillery. The royal party then enters the Palace of Westminster through the Victoria Tower. The Queen walks upstairs to the Robing Room and from there emerges wearing her magnificent crown. She is then led by heralds into the House of Lords, where her appearance is announced by trumpeters. The Lords in all their finery are already present. The Commons are now summoned (by an official known as the Gentleman Usher of the Black Rod) and these commoners – including the Prime Minister and the Cabinet – stand to listen to the 'Queen's Speech', which sets out the government's policy for the following parliamentary year.

Before the ceremony, the vaults of the Houses of Parliament will have been searched by the Yeomen of the Guard, a search that has been carried out every year since 1605, when the Gunpowder Plot, Guy Fawkes's attempt to blow up the Palace of Westminster, failed.

The Nation's Spiritual Heart

Westminster Abbey, is the spiritual heart of the British people, as St Paul's is the spiritual heart of London. For nearly 1,000 years, all the kings and queens of England, with the exception of Edward V and Edward VIII, have been crowned in Westminster Abbey, and it is in this great church that many of them are buried. The abbey is also the last resting-place of many of Britain's most famous citizens and it has been the setting for numerous royal weddings, including those of the present Queen and Queen Mother, and of royal funerals – most recently that of Diana, Princess of Wales.

It is fitting that a church so embedded in the national conscience should have had a legendary beginning. In the 7th century, a little church newly built on the Isle of Thorney (now Westminster) was consecrated by the first Bishop of London. The night before the consecration, a hooded man asked a poor fisherman to ferry him across the river to the church. When they were halfway across, the fisherman saw that the church was bathed in a dazzling light and heard the singing of a heavenly choir. The stranger threw back his hood, revealing himself as St Peter. He consecrated the church and rewarded the fisherman with a huge catch of salmon, promising him that there would always be plentiful fish for him and his successors in the river as long as he gave a tithe to the church and did not fish on Sundays.

What is undoubtedly true is that there was already a church on the site – the abbey of a Benedictine monastery – when Edward the Confessor became king in 1042. He had vowed to make a pilgrimage to Rome, but affairs of state prevented the journey and the Pope released him from his vow on condition that he built a new Benedictine monastery to St Peter at Westminster. Edward built

a grand new church, which he lived just long enough to see consecrated in December 1065. He died eight days later, on 5 January 1066, and was buried before the high altar. That year was a momentous one for England: it saw the succession of Harold to the throne (he may have been crowned in the abbey) before his defeat at the Battle of Hastings and the coronation on Christmas Day of his conqueror, William of Normandy, in Westminster Abbey. It was this coronation that set the precedent that has been followed ever since.

Little remains of Edward the Confessor's church. The present building was begun in 1245 by Henry III. The eastern end, completed by 1269, is the finest example of early English Gothic architecture in the country and, at a height of 31 metres (103 feet), is taller than any other church of the period in Britain. We have Richard II's architect Henry Yevele to thank for the fact that the nave, though completed over 100 years later, is in the same style, giving the abbey its wonderful sense of unity.

Kings and their families, from Henry III to George II, were buried close to the high altar, and for centuries interment in the abbey has been considered the greatest honour that the nation can bestow on its citizens. The abbey is crowded with grand monuments and tombs to people now forgotten, but the greatest are still remembered and many of them are buried in groups or clusters. Visitors come from all over the world to pay tribute to the likes of Isaac Newton and other famous thinkers in Scientists' Corner, to visit Musicians' Aisle to see the tomb of Henry Purcell, and Radicals' Corner to see the great reformers and pioneers of the socialist movement. Statesmen are also remembered here, in Politicians' Aisle, but most of

Detail of the southwest side of the abbey, showing some typically Gothic architectural features, including, on the left, a flying buttress.

all visitors come to honour the greatest of English poets and writers buried or commemorated in Poets' Corner. Geoffrey Chaucer, Edmund Spenser, Tennyson, Byron, Keats, Wordsworth, Jane Austen, D. H. Lawrence, T. S. Eliot, William Shakespeare (his memorial was not put up until 1740), Wilfred Owen, the Brontë Sisters, Charles Dickens and Thomas Hardy are a few among many. Other burials or commemorations are to be found scattered apparently at random through the church. Look hard and you will find David Livingstone, the African missionary and explorer and Ben Jonson, Shakespeare's great rival, in the nave (Jonson is supposed to have been buried standing up). More recent theatrical figures commemorated include Noel Coward, in the south choir aisle, and Laurence Olivier, in the south transept, along with George Frederick Handel.

The Tomb of the Unknown Warrior

Yet perhaps the most important, and certainly the most moving, of all the tombs in the abbey is that of a man who gave his life for his country in the First World War. Just to the east of the west door, close to the memorial to Winston Churchill, is the tomb of the Unknown Warrior. The soldier will never be identified, but he represents the many thousands who gave their lives in that bloody and barbaric war. No one ever walks on this most honoured grave: processions split in two to file past. The tomb is surrounded by poppies, the flowers that will for ever be associated with the battlefields of France. The burial took place on 11 November 1920, exactly two years after the end of the First World War. The funeral was attended by the King, the Prime Minister, members of his cabinet and the service chiefs. The guard of honour was made up of 100 soldiers who had been awarded the Victoria Cross, Britain's highest military award. The coffin was buried in earth that had been brought from the battlefields of France and covered by a slab of Belgian marble. On a nearby column hangs the Congressional

The Lord Mayor's coach, built in 1757, on its annual outing. When not in use in the Lord Mayor's Show every November, it can be found in the Museum of London at the Barbican, where its magnificent decoration by Cipriani may be admired more closely.

Medal of Honour, the highest military distinction of the United States, bestowed upon the Unknown Warrior in 1921. Thus all the allies joined in honouring him. Close by hangs the 'Padre's Flag', which had been used to cover the graves of many soldiers buried in France and was laid over that of the Unknown Warrior at his burial.

Today the official title of Westminster Abbey is the Collegiate Church of St Peter in Westminster. The Benedictine Monastery was dissolved in 1540, and the abbey survived only because of its royal associations. Part of the church's revenues were transferred to St Paul's Cathedral, thus giving rise to the expression 'robbing Peter to pay Paul'. The church was created a 'royal peculiar'- a

church directly responsible to the monarch instead of to a bishop – by Elizabeth I in 1560. It has been a royal peculiar ever since, controlled by the Dean and Chapter in the name of the monarch.

A Grand Procession

Compared to Westminster, there is rather less public ceremonial in the City, but the great exception is the Lord Mayor's Show, which is watched by thousands. Surprisingly, it takes place when the weather is likely to mar enjoyment, on the second Saturday of November, when the City would have been left to cats and caretakers. The show marks the moment when the newly elected mayor publicly takes office. He progresses from Mansion House, his official home at Bank, to the Royal Courts of Justice in the Strand to take his oath of office before the Judges of the Queen's Bench.

The Lord Mayor's Show dates back to the 13th century, when the Lord Mayor presented himself before the king at Westminster for approval, and to 'swear fealty'. For three centuries mayors travelled by river to Westminster in a magnificent

ABOVE The Lord Mayor's Procession making its way to the Royal Courts of Justice where the new Lord Mayor will oficially and very publicly take office. This show, is perhaps the most spectacular of all the annual ceremonies in the City of London.

RIGHT The Veteran Car Run is one of the annual highlights for lovers of old cars. All year the vehicles have been polished and pampered and now they are ready to travel the 60 miles to Madeira Drive in Brighton.

barge with silver oars. In later years he rode on horseback for part of the procession – until 1711, when Sir Gilbert Heathcote was unsaddled by a drunken flower girl! Since then, the Mayor has travelled by coach. The present coach has been in use since 1757.

The pageantry has increased in splendour over the years. City poets provided a feast of themed entertainment and members of the Livery Companies dressed up in their finest. In 1602 the grand procession included a 'Lyon and a camel'. In the pageant of 1672 a throned Indian emperor rode with princes of Peru and Mexico at his feet: 'Two extra great giants each of them fifteen feet high were drawn by horses in two separate chariots,

moving, talking and taking tobacco as they rode along to the great admiration and delight of all spectators.' The celebrations were not always noted for their restraint, however, and one year the route was packed on either side by cheering crowds, who pelted the better dressed with rubbish.

Today the whole affair is more seemly, with the theme each year being chosen by the incoming Lord Mayor. Recent themes have included such worthy subjects as 'Natural Resources and the Environment' and 'Moving ahead with Europe'. The spectacle, now rather more decorous than in the past, is still enjoyed by the thousands of spectators who arrive early in the morning to gain a good vantage point along the route. The day is rounded off with a fireworks display.

Off to Brighton!

The Veteran Car Run also provides free entertainment each November. It was first held in 1896, when the law stating that all vehicles must be preceded by a man carrying a red flag was repealed. Starting very early in the morning at Hyde Park Corner, a line of magnificent old cars, each made before 31 December 1904, begins to form. The cars set off in batches, amid much tooting, honking and backfiring, on their 96.5-kilometre (60-mile) journey to Brighton on the south coast. Many will not complete the course – some may not get going at all – but it is the taking part that counts. And there is always next year to try again.

'London, thou art the flower of cities all!
Gemme of all joy, jasper of jocunditie.'
WILLIAM DUNBAR

London Breaks for

Lunch

There are times of day when London's streets are ant-hill crowded. Noon and for a couple of hours after is such a time: the streets have been bustling all morning with visitors and now the offices release tides of employees who spend their lunch-hour either eating or enjoying one of the huge variety of pastimes that the metropolis has to offer.

There is much to occupy the Londoner and the visitor during the middle of the day. Some will indulge in 'retail therapy' – psychobabble for shopping or window-gazing. Others, more practically, will spend their precious lunch-hour buying the ingredients for the evening meal in one of central London's street markets. Many of the larger and some of the smaller museums and art galleries offer lunch-time talks or tours, timed to allow people to grab a bite to eat, attend the event and get back to work for the afternoon. There are also lunch-time concerts, suitably timed, in many churches and parks.

The Business Lunch

Some folk will simply wish to share their hour with friends or colleagues. All over London, restaurants, cafés, sandwich bars and pubs are packed. Of course, not all lunches are taken purely for pleasure. The 'business lunch', which often takes rather longer than an hour, is to be observed in some of the grand old restaurants. In Simpsons in the Strand or in Rules in Maiden Lane, for example, sharp businessman entertains sharp businessman over roast beef and Yorkshire pudding or steak and kidney pie. Advertising executives and film folk also believe in taking their time over lunch with clients. They are to be found in the trendy eateries of Soho nibbling on their roasted peppers and fettucini.

The cosmopolitan nature of Covent Garden is clearly demonstrated in this view of Catherine Street, showing a traditional pub, an Indian restaurant and a French restaurant. These establishments, which are just opposite the Theatre Royal, Drury Lane, and those in the surrounding streets, serve both shoppers and theatre-goers.

ABOVE A spreading chestnut tree in Hyde Park. This is the largest of the central parks, which, together with Kensington Gardens, forms a continuous open space of 243 hectares (600 acres). The Serpentine was created out of a series of ponds in 1730 for Queen Caroline, the wife of George II, and extends into Kensington Gardens. It is used for boating and bathing. From the Serpentine Bridge there is a fine view of the distant Palace of Westminster and Westminster Abbey.

Dining Alfresco

In fine weather, every pocket of open space is filled with people sitting on park benches, on the grass and on walls, all eating their sandwiches in the open air. Even in the City, where there are few open spaces, tiny gardens have been created out of bombed churches or old graveyards and are filled with workers enjoying the quiet. One such place is Tower Hill, where once heads fell at the drop of an axe but now is the lunch-time meeting place for head-hunters and their quarry. For those who find physical exercise relaxing, there are walks to be taken by the river or along the Regent's Canal.

Quieter Moments

The churches within the City of London come into their own at lunch-time. There are too many of them for the religious needs of the tiny population of the City, and although their primary purpose is worship, many of them are used, especially at lunch-time, for concerts, theatre and talks. Here, esoteric societies meet, the great old Livery Companies hold ceremonies and some-times their peaceful isolation within the throbbing city offers solace to the troubled or weary, who can pause within them before stepping back into the fray.

BELOW LEFT Although there are many benches provided for the use of the public in Hyde Park and elsewhere, when the weather is hot, people prefer to relax on the grass.

BELOW Deck-chairs in Green Park. Once the art of erecting a deck-chair has been mastered, it makes a very comfortable seat. Contrary to popular belief, however, the deck-chairs in London's parks are not supplied free. Just as you have settled down for a lunch-time snooze, an attendant will come and ask you to pay for its use!

Some people will simply spend time in the middle of the day enjoying the amazing architectural feast that these churches present. The majority are the work of Sir Christopher Wren and were built to replace earlier churches burned down in the Great Fire of London of 1666. Even though many Wren churches were destroyed during the Second World War, enough remain to demonstrate the huge talent of Britain's greatest architect. Each church is different, representing Wren's imaginative solution to the problems presented by awkward, asymmetrical, cramped sites. In most he experimented – with domes and spires and other architectural innovations. In one, he responded

LEFT The delightful spire of St Bride, which has been called 'a madrigal in stone', is all that remains of Sir Christopher Wren's church after it was bombed during the Second World War; the rest of the church is the result of restoration work carried out in the 1950s. Wren's church was not the first on the site and in the crypt can be seen evidence of the earlier buildings and of Roman London.

St Bride's Church stands just off Fleet Street – Mr Rich, a pastry cook who lived in Fleet Street used the spire as a model for the wedding cakes that made him famous – and has connections with newspapers and writers. Samuel Pepys, the 17th-century diarist, was baptized here, and Samuel Richardson, 'father of the English novel', was buried in the church. It was also the campaign centre for the Friends of John McCarthy – the British journalist who was held hostage in Lebanon from 1986 to 1991.

ABOVE St Michael Paternoster Royal is another of the 51 churches
in the City of London that Wren rebuilt after the Great Fire
of 1666. The previous church on the site was built by Dick
Whittington, thrice Lord Mayor of London, who was buried
here in 1423. There is a delightful modern stained-glass window
showing Whittington's famous cat. Although the church was
bombed in 1944, much of the fine interior woodwork survives.

LEFT St Mary-le-Bow on Cheapside is often called Bow Church
and genuine cockneys are supposed to have been born within
the sound of its bells. Difficult today, surrounded as it is by offices,
with not a home or hospital in sight! Christopher Wren was
responsible for the beautiful campanile and for the steeple, which
is surmounted by a weather-vane in the form of a dragon – the
symbol of the City. The church stands above a Norman crypt
of the late 11th century, in which the principal ecclesiastical court
– the Court of Arches (or bows) was held until 1847.

OVERLEAF A view of St Paul's Cathedral from the river.
In front of it stands the old City of London School (the current
school buildings are now a little further east) and on the river is
the HMS President, a former training ship which is permanently
moored here.

with great sensitivity, accommodating the original style of the Gothic church that he was rebuilding. Even now that the skyline of the City is no longer punctuated by his spires and cupolas, concealed as they are by the high-rise office blocks built after the war, and St Paul's no longer has the same dominant profile as it once did, it is still possible to discern his vision.

A Symbol of London

London's cathedral may no longer dominate the City's skyline but it is still the capital's spiritual heart. For over 1,000 years Londoners have gathered here to worship, to celebrate great national events, to mourn the passing of its leaders. More recent years have also seen City workers relaxing on the grass in the cathedral's grounds, basking in the mid-day sunshine during the lunch-hour.

St Paul's is a symbol of London, and never more potently so than during the Second World War, when it was felt that if St Paul's could survive, so could London. Each morning after a night of heavy bombing, weary folk would look up to the dome and feel a little more secure when they saw that it still towered over the ravaged city.

There has been a church on this site for 14 centuries, and it is possible that there was a Roman temple here even before that. The first Saxon church, a small wooden structure built in 604, was destroyed by fire and raids. Its early replacements suffered similar fates. The present St Paul's immediate predecessor was magnificent: Old St Paul's dated from 1087 but was largely a Gothic building, and almost twice the size of today's church. Until it was struck by lightning in

The west front of St Paul's Cathedral. In the triangular pediment is a bas relief by Francis Bird portraying the conversion of St Paul. The statues above the pediment are also by Bird and depict St Paul in the middle, with St Peter to the left and St James to the right. The north-west Tower to the left houses the cathedral bells.

Queen Anne, whose statue stands in front of St Paul's, was the monarch when the church was completed in 1710. This statue is a 19th-century copy of the original by Francis Bird, who was responsible, under Wren, for much of the carving around the Cathedral.

1561, the spire of this church was a wonder of the medieval world, standing over 30 metres (about 100 feet) higher than today's dome. Inside the church stood the magnificent tombs of John of Gaunt and Philip Sidney. Its walls had reverberated to the service of celebration attended by Queen Elizabeth I following England's victory over the Spanish Armada. However, Old St Paul's, famous though it was, was a neglected building, often abused. Dealers traded in the nave and animals were led through the church, which was used as a short cut from one part of the city to another. During the Civil War it was used as a barracks for Cromwell's troops. Horses were stabled in the church and their manure was sold to market gardens around the city! Those eternal

pests of London, pigeons, if they trespassed inside, were shot, predictably causing damage to the stained glass windows.

Old St Paul's was one of the many casualties of the Great Fire of London of 1666, much to the amazement of Londoners of the day, who had thought that it was indestructible. So bad was the damage that only one monument survived – the tomb of the metaphysical poet John Donne, who had been Dean of St Paul's. It can be seen today in the south choir aisle of the present church, the marble a little singed at the base.

Plainly, St Paul's had to be rebuilt, and the architect chosen was Christopher Wren. His brief was to produce a church of low cost. His first design was considered much too small, and his

LONDON BREAKS FOR LUNCH 109

second too modern. In order to help the authorities visualize what he intended he made a magnificent model in wood to illustrate his next design. The Great Model still exists, looking similar but not the same as the building that now stands. This design, too, was rejected. There were fears that it would be too similar to St Peter's in Rome, and therefore too popish. In disgust, Wren produced another design, which has subsequently been described as the worst design ever submitted by a great architect. An uneasy mixture of the Gothic and the baroque, this was the one that was finally accepted! Fortunately, when King Charles II issued his warrant of approval he stated that Wren was 'to make some Variations, rather ornamental, than essential, as from Time to Time he should see proper; and to leave the Whole to his own Management'. This gave the architect the freedom he needed. The present cathedral bears very little resemblance to the approved design, which did not even have a dome.

When the site had been cleared in preparation for the rebuilding, Wren asked one of his workmen to bring him a stone to mark the centre of the church. By chance, the stone he was given was a fragment of a gravestone from the old church. On it was one word – *Resurgam*, meaning 'I will rise again'. Wren was so moved by this that over the entrance to the south transept he placed a sculpture of a phoenix rising from the ashes, with the word '*Resurgam*' below it.

St Paul's was built between 1675 and 1710. Wren was busy on many other projects during its construction – he was responsible for rebuilding 50 other City churches – but he supervised all stages of the work. As the dome began to emerge from behind the wattle screen that surrounded the site, he would be hoisted in a basket to the top to inspect progress every Saturday. In 1708, aged 76, he watched as his own son fixed the last stone into position at the traditional 'topping out ceremony'.

St Paul's dome, one of the largest in the world, is a masterpiece of construction. It is, in fact, three structures: the exterior dome, which is clad in

lead, the smaller interior dome and, between the two, a brick cone that supports the weight of the lantern. The dome stands on eight great piers linked by eight arches and weighs 65,000 tonnes. The golden cross at the top stands 111 metres (about 365 feet) from the ground.

Wren was an old man by the time St Paul's was completed. Work did not always proceed smoothly and progress was often slow. He had troubles and disagreements with the Commissioners and at one stage his salary was halved. But he worshipped often in the new cathedral and it was after one service that he returned home and died peacefully in a chair by his fireside. He was in his 91st year. He is buried in the cathedral but, unlike Wellington and Nelson and many other famous and less famous Englishmen, he has no elaborate memorial in the church. His grave in the crypt is plain, but on the wall above it is a marble tablet that bears the words *Lector, si monumentum requiris circumspice*, which translate as: 'Reader, if his monument you seek, look around you.'

RIGHT The dome of St Paul's – symbol of London's survival in the Second World War. The cathedral was saved from fire bombs by St Paul's Watch, who are commemorated by a plaque in the nave. This band of volunteers, which included the poet Sir John Betjeman, patrolled the roof area each night and by their vigilance prevented the lead-clad dome from catching fire.

LEFT A colourful scene in Covent Garden. The area is full of eccentrics who entertain the crowds throughout the day. Here, at a bric-à-brac stall in Apple Market, a man dressed as a town crier, in scarlet cloak and plumed hat is causing some interest!

RIGHT In the central hall of Covent Garden crowds gather to listen to a recital by a string quartet. Some have found seats, but many more hang over the gallery to enjoy the music.

RIGHT On a fine summer's day the umbrellas at Tuttons in Covent Garden provide welcome shade for diners. This restaurant is just around the corner from the Theatre Museum and is next door to the Transport Museum.

Lunch-time Entertainment

There are some parts of London that seem to have been specially designed for the lunch-hour: Covent Garden comes into its own now, and will remain vibrant well into the evening. Today, the area is the centre of the theatre district, but long before the first playhouses were built, the land belonged to the monks of Westminster Abbey. It was their 'convent' garden. When Henry VIII dissolved the monasteries in the middle of the 16th century the land became his to dispose of. It was granted by the Crown to the 1st Earl of Bedford. Later, the 4th Earl commissioned Inigo Jones to lay out a piazza, or square (the first such design in London), with a church on one side and tall terraced houses on the other three sides, an arrangement that the Londoners of the day found very peculiar and foreign. Initially, the houses were taken by the rich and aristocratic, but they soon moved west to the new and more fashionable developments around St James's Palace.

The spread of the market in the centre of the

square had done nothing to encourage them to stay. The market had begun in 1670, when the 5th Earl of Bedford was granted a charter to hold a market of flowers, fruit, roots and herbs in Covent Garden. As the market expanded, houses and shops were built around it and coffee shops sprang up in the vicinity, becoming meeting-places for the writers and intellectuals of the day. During the 18th century Covent Garden became increasingly the haunt of actors and artists and, notoriously, of prostitutes. Sir Henry Fielding, playwright, novelist and magistrate, called it 'the great square of Venus'. The epony-mous heroine of *Fanny Hill* had lodgings in the market where 'provided the rent was duly paid, everything else was as easy and commodious as one could desire'.

By the beginning of the 19th century the market had become chaotic and congested. Attempts were made to improve matters by building a market hall. This building, which dates from the early 1830s, still exists and forms the centre-piece of what is the Covent Garden of today. Through the 19th century, and well into the 20th, Covent Garden was a colourful market where fashionable Londoners enjoyed mingling with farmers, costermongers and flowergirls – a

relationship famously explored by George Bernard Shaw in *Pygmalion*, when Eliza Doolittle and Professor Higgins meet under the portico of Covent Garden's own St Paul's Church, famous today as the actor's church. However, it became increasingly difficult for large delivery vehicles (often from distant corners of Europe) to gain access to the market and, after 200 years, the market finally closed in 1974. 'New Covent Garden' is now a few miles away, at Nine Elms on the south side of the river.

Happily, the lovely old market buildings were retained in the redevelopment of Covent Garden that followed. The old buildings now house shops, restaurants, cafés and pubs, but there are still stalls selling all manner of goods – crafts, bric-à-brac and antiques, though not fruit and vegetables – and the lively market atmosphere has been preserved. But it is mainly a place of entertainment. From lunch-time until late in the evening, every type of enter-tainment – from fire-eating to classical music concerts – can be enjoyed in the open air. Most of the entertainers are unknowns who will never emerge from obscurity, but one or two started in the piazza and went on to become stars – the most dazzling of them, to date, is undoubtedly the comedian Eddie Izzard.

The Long Afternoon

*I*t is afternoon, and the streets are filled with visitors making their leisurely way from one attraction to another, pausing to feed the pigeons in Trafalgar Square, or taking in the atmosphere of Piccadilly Circus and Leicester Square a short distance away. Some may explore further afield by pleasure boat, travelling downstream to the Tower of London and beyond it to Greenwich. Others may cruise upstream to Kew Gardens and Hampton Court.

Well-kept Secrets

There is so much to enjoy in London that the visitor is spoilt for choice. No wonder so many come once and then return again and again. Those who have been to London before may now be seeking out the less well-known spots to enjoy. The Wallace Collection, tucked away just behind Oxford Street, is such a place – few enough people go to Hertford House in Manchester Square to visit this outstanding museum and art gallery. Those who do find their way there will see one of the finest collections of Sèvres porcelain in the country, a magnificent collection of French 18th-century furniture and a feast of paintings by the Old Masters, including Franz Hals's *The Laughing Cavalier*. And there is room upon room of arms and armour.

The Geffrye Museum, situated in unpromising surroundings amid forbidding modern high-rise social housing in Shoreditch, is housed in delightful almshouses, happy survivors from the 18th century. Inside, each room is furnished in the style of a different era. For the connoisseur of English furniture through the ages there is no better place to visit. It is a museum for the student of social life and mores.

Rather grander 18th-century architecture can be seen between two of London's 'villages', Hampstead and Highgate. Kenwood House, designed by

LEFT Robert Adam's gem, Kenwood House, seen from Hampstead Heath. Anyone who likes walking can enjoy this delightful view, thanks to the local inhabitants, who fought long and hard to save the heath from developers in the 19th and early 20th centuries. Today the heath covers some 320 hectares (about 800 acres) and is hugely popular with Londoners, especially on bank holidays, when a funfair draws huge crowds.

ABOVE The view made famous by Canaletto, who painted Greenwich from the Isle of Dogs when he visited London in the 1750s. In the centre is the Queen's House – the first Palladian building in England – designed by Inigo Jones for Queen Anne, wife of James I. Closer to the river and flanking the Queen's House are several blocks of what was to have been a new royal palace. However, William and Mary decided to turn it into a home or hospital for old sailors, to match the hospital for soldiers upstream at Chelsea. It is now a college. The Queen's House is today a museum and the buildings on either side of it form part of the National Maritime Museum.

LEFT Chiswick House was built by Lord Burlington in the grounds of his then principle residence as 'a temple to the arts'. The gardens were laid out by William Kent, and were filled with sculpture, temples and obelisks, in the Italian style.

RIGHT The Chinese Pagoda in Kew Gardens was built by Sir William Chambers in 1761, as a surprise for Princess Augusta. Formed originally as gardens for two royal palaces, Kew is today concerned primarily with research into plants from all over the world. The gardens are beautiful throughout the year, but are perhaps most visited by Londoners in the spring, when the bluebells are a wonderful sight.

Robert Adam for Lord Mansfield, a judge, now houses the small but magnificent Iveagh Bequest of paintings, including one of Rembrandt's last self-portraits and a little jewel of a painting by Vermeer. The sight of Kenwood, approached from across Hampstead Heath and sparkling in the sunlight, is one of the most attractive in London.

West London – the preferred side of town for most aristocrats because the river afforded easy access to the capital – has a number of grand houses. One of the most interesting, set in lovely landscaped gardens, is Chiswick House. Lord Burlington, an enthusiast of all the arts, designed the mansion himself, with some help from William Kent, in a style imitating that of the 16th-century Italian architect Andrea Palladio. Burlington did not intend to live in it – there were no bedrooms and no kitchen – but rather to use it for entertaining and showing off the fine collection of statuary, paintings, urns and Roman tombs he had acquired

LEFT Sir John Soane's Museum in Lincoln's Inn Fields. This was the private home of the famous architect. When he died, he stipulated in his will that none of the pieces in his collection should be disturbed or added to, therefore the house looks exactly as it did on the day of his death in 1837.

during his Grand Tour. The treasures are said to have filled some 800 crates on their journey back to England.

Back in the centre of town is Sir John Soane's Museum, another little-known delight. Sir John Soane was an architect of the late 18th and early 19th centuries, whose austere buildings have largely disappeared. The curtain wall of the Bank of England, a church and the Dulwich Art Gallery, also well worth a visit, remain, but little else. However, the curious house that he designed for himself in Lincoln's Inn Fields, between Holborn and Fleet

design for the Houses of Parliament.

The Courtauld Institute Galleries are to be found in part of the 18th-century Somerset House, which stands beside Waterloo Bridge overlooking the Thames. The collection is not large, but includes magnificent baroque, impressionist and post-impressionist paintings. There are fine examples of the work of Rubens, Manet, Renoir, Monet, Van Gogh and Gauguin among them. Many of these paintings are familiar from countless reproductions, but it comes as a revelation to many visitors to see them in actuality.

ABOVE A pleasure cruiser makes its leisurely way past Shellmex House. This huge building occupies an entire block from the Strand to Embankment. When it first opened as the Cecil Hotel in 1886 it had 800 bedrooms and was the largest hotel in Europe. Its riverside façade with enormous clock was remodelled in 1931.

Street, which he filled with treasures displaying his wide interests, survives. It is one of the smaller collections in London, but a gem for all that. As a result of his difficult relationship with his sons, Soane did not leave the house to his children, but to the nation. The house contains everything from Egyptian sarcophagi and Greek statuary to the works of William Hogarth, including the artist's famous sequence of paintings, *A Rake's Progress*. Soane's interest in light and the different ways in which it can be brought into a room is magically demonstrated with the use of mirrors, unexpected windows and skylights. There are many architectural drawings and models on display, notably his

Tower of London

Another of London's most enduring tourist attractions, and one which deserves a whole afternoon dedicated to exploring its extraordinary history – which stretches back over 900 years – is the Tower of London. The most perfect example of a medieval fortress in Britain, it has been a royal palace, an arsenal, a royal menagerie, a royal mint, a prison and a place of execution. It still houses the Crown Jewels and is home to some 40 Yeomen Warders, whose job it is to look after the building and the visitors. On most days they wear their 'undress' uniform of blue, which was devised in

The Pool of London, with the Tower of London on the left and Tower Bridge, spanning the Thames, to the right. The central section of the bridge can be raised like a double drawbridge to enable tall ships to pass through. The top crossing was originally a pedestrian walkway open to the elements, but is now glassed over and is part of the Tower Bridge Museum.

the 19th century, but on special occasions they are dressed in scarlet and gold, the royal livery of Henry VIII.

After William I was crowned in Westminster Abbey on Christmas Day 1066 he withdrew to Essex 'while certain strongholds were made in the city against the fickleness of the vast and fierce population for he realised that it was of the first importance to overawe the Londoners. The Tower of London is the only one of these strongholds that survives. By the end of William's reign the great central keep, the White Tower, was probably well on the way to completion and stood, massive and dominant, on the south-east edge of the city,

ready to serve as a London power base for the king and as a stronghold for the royal family in times of civil unrest.

By 1350 successive enlargements had resulted in the outline of the Tower we see today. The whole edifice was surrounded by a moat filled with swirling water which was not drained until the middle of the 19th century. Not surprisingly, this massive fortification has never in its history been taken by force.

One of the oddest things to have had a home in this military fortress was the royal menagerie. It all began in 1235 when Henry III was given three leopards. The collection swiftly grew. In 1252 the

Sherriffs of London were ordered to buy a chain for the polar bear (a gift from the King of Norway) so that he could be taken fishing in the River Thames! The menagerie moved out of its dungeon-like accommodation in the now-demolished Lion Tower only when the London Zoo was founded in 1834. The only creatures that remain in the Tower are the ravens. There is a legend which says that if the ravens ever leave, the Tower will fall and with it the nation. To ensure this never comes to pass, a minimum of six of these great black birds are kept within its walls. The ravens are thus considered very important and have a specially appointed warder to look after them. Housed in luxurious accommoda-

tion, they live much longer than they would in the wild. The clipping of their wings is the price they pay for their longevity.

The Crown Jewels

Today, most people go to the Tower primarily to see the Crown Jewels. These magnificent gems – in crowns, rings, sceptres and orbs – have been on display in the Tower for centuries, although their security has not always been taken as seriously as it is today. In 1671, the jewels were stolen by a Thomas Blood. He was apprehended on Tower Wharf, more by luck than any real

The English Regalia is used at the coronation of each monarch. In the centre is the Crown of St Edward, with which each new monarch is crowned. To the left is the oldest piece, the anointing spoon which dates from the twelfth century, and at the front is the sceptre containing the First Star of Africa, the largest diamond in the world weighing 530 carats.

judgement. In 1815, a madwoman got hold of the State Crown and wrenched it apart, causing considerable damage. When the jewels were housed in the Wakefield Tower, they were displayed in a great cage and, if you asked nicely, the Yeoman Warder on duty might be prepared to unlock the cage and let you try on one of the crowns!

The most famous of all the jewels is probably the First Star of Africa, the biggest diamond in the world. It was cut from the Cullinan diamond which had been found by a mine worker in 1905, and was given to King Edward VII by the Transvaal government. The Second Star of Africa can also be seen in the Imperial State Crown. Then there is the Koh-i-noor diamond which, according to legend, must only be worn by a

woman, the Balas Ruby, which was given to the Black Prince in 1367 and worn on his helmet by Henry V at the battle of Agincourt and pearls said to have been earrings of Queen Elizabeth I. No wonder visitors wait patiently to see these treasures.

Today, the Tower of London presents a benign face to tourists, especially in summer when it is full to bursting and every language under the sun is to be heard. Consider a night visit too, to witness the ancient Ceremony of the Keys, or go early one weekday morning in winter, when it is cold and grey, and you can more easily people it in your imagination with names that echo down the centuries – the names of kings, queens, princes and bishops who have been imprisoned in the

Tower, some only leaving to go to their execution.

The place is full of ghosts. Imagine Sir Thomas More, confined for months in the Bell Tower, or Princess Elizabeth, daughter of Henry VIII, terrified, as she passed under Traitors Gate, that she would suffer the same fate as her mother Ann Boleyn and her cousin Lady Jane Grey and meet her death within the Tower. Or imagine the same Elizabeth returning in triumph to the Tower after her succession to the throne. Imagine, also, the little 'Princes in the Tower' Edward V and his brother Richard dying by the hand of person or persons unknown, murdered in the Tower, or Guy Fawkes fearfully awaiting his next appointment with the torturer. Or Henry VI, founder of Eton and King's College, Cambridge, who was killed while at his prayers. Imagine, more happily, medieval coronation days, when the populace gathered outside the Tower to cheer their new monarch on his way to Westminster Abbey and

the conduits of the city ran with wine. Imagine the Scottish Lord Nithsdale escaping from the Tower disguised as a woman, concealing his great red beard behind a handkerchief. Or imagine the Yeomen Warders tending their vegetables in the moat-turned-allotment during the Second World War. Sitting proud on the River Thames, so much of England's history is to be found in the Tower that no-one should pass it by.

A Riverside Walk

The afternoon is a time when much entertainment takes place in the capital. There are matinées at the West End theatres and, in the summer months, concerts on bandstands in the parks, where many gather to sit in the striped deck-chairs or on the grass. In recent years entertainment has expanded from the West End to the South Bank. The expansion began with the Festival of Britain in 1951, when the

Royal Festival Hall was built as part of the celebrations. Today it is just one part of the enormous complex known as the South Bank Arts Centre, which includes the prestigious Hayward Art Gallery, the Royal National Theatre, the National Film Theatre and the Museum of the Moving Image.

A pleasant afternoon walk can be taken along the South Bank, from Westminster to Bankside. Just beyond Westminster Bridge stands County Hall, once the headquarters of the Greater London Council and, before that, of the London County Council. Both these institutions are now gone and the huge building is home to the

ABOVE The Royal Festival Hall is one of the capital's premier concert halls and is home to two of London's major symphony orchestras, the London Philharmonic and the Philharmonia. The main stage can hold a choir of 250. There is, in addition, a small recital room. The building also contains a large foyer, where exhibitions are held, and several eating areas, including the People's Palace Restaurant, which overlooks the river.

RIGHT The Royal National Theatre, or the NT as it invariably bills itself, opened in 1976. The idea for a national theatre was first seriously mooted in 1848, but its gestation was long and painful and this site was not chosen until 1944. The foundation stone was laid in 1951 but building, to the design of Denys Lasdun, did not begin until 1969. Today the theatre, with its three auditoria, is very successful and the National Theatre Company is generally considered the finest in the country.

London Aquarium, the FA Premier League Hall of Fame, two hotels and some luxury apartments. Beyond County Hall, one can take a comfortable embankment stroll to Waterloo Bridge. Under the bridge there is a small book market and close by, at certain times, free entertainment in Theatre Square in front of the National Theatre.

Until a few years ago, the South Bank Arts Centre was an oasis of culture set amid a depressing and depressed desert of offices, decaying factories and bombsites. Now, in the area beyond the National Theatre, a transformation has taken place, brought about by the determination of the people who live in the neighbourhood. There were plans to rebuild the whole 5-hectare (about 13 acres) site with huge office blocks and hotels, restricting access to the Thames. It seemed an obvious choice as a site for redevelopment: the population had dwindled from 50,000 in 1900 to 5,000 by the 1970s and shops and schools were closing. But the remaining residents refused to be forced out. They formed themselves into the Coin Street Action Group and put forward an alternative plan. After two public enquiries, they won the day. The area has been transformed and more improvements are to come. Now the walk can continue along the river past

RIGHT This stretch of river is known as King's Reach. The foreground area has only recently become accessible to the public and is already much appreciated. In the distance, to the right, is the Oxo Tower, with Blackfriars Bridge beyond.

Gabriel's Wharf, where craftsmen making and selling their wares do a roaring trade. The multi-cultural Coin Street Festival ensures that, in the summer, the area is vibrant, the streets and open spaces on occasion filled with dancers, banners, music and exhibitions of every imaginable kind. The people who work in the surrounding office blocks, who would in the past have stayed indoors all day and left the area in a hurry at night, now enjoy, with the residents, the new spirit of community that is tangible even to the casual passer-by.

ABOVE The new Globe Theatre was the first building in London to be allowed a thatched roof since the Great Fire of London of 1666. Sam Wanamaker, the American actor, dreamed of building a replica of Shakespeare's theatre close to its original site, and battled for years with councils and planners, and was always short of money. He prevailed in the end but, sadly, died before the building was finished.

The new development includes a pretty park and, beyond it, the Oxo building, with its eccentric landmark tower. The lower floors of the building are devoted to the selling of exquisite handcrafted goods, the middle floor to social housing and the top to a viewing platform and one of the most fashionable restaurants in London.

Emerging from under Blackfriars Bridge, the walker is confronted by the great bulk of what was once a coal-fired power station. It is now the Tate Modern Gallery, home of the national collection of modern art. The walk ends triumphantly at the

This historical photograph
shows fans leaving Wembley
Stadium after one of the
last games ever played there.
There were hopes that the
twin towers would be
retained on the new stadium,
but the architect, Norman
Foster, was not prepared to
incorporate them in his
design, promising a great
arch instead.

new Globe Theatre in Southwark, which is
crowded with audiences experiencing Shakespeare
in a facsimile of the theatre he knew so well.

Good Sports

The afternoon is also when most of the major
sporting events take place. Wembley Stadium,
soon to be rebuilt, is one of the best-known and
best-loved sports arenas in the world. The most
important football fixtures are played at Wembley
and fans converge on London from all over the
country to watch the national team or their local
club compete. For domestic and international football, Wembley is almost a shrine and tickets for
important matches change hands for hundreds of
pounds. English supporters still talk of the World
Cup Final that took place at Wembley in 1966,
which England won in a nail-biting finish. The
headquarters of Rugby Football is in another distant
suburb of London – Twickenham. Here, equally passionate fans gather to watch international matches.
The Twickenham crowds are ebullient enough, but

less rowdy than those at football matches.

London has two cricket grounds, Lord's and the
Oval, where both county and international cricket
are played throughout the summer months. By
afternoon the games are well under way, and the
teams will be thinking about a drinks break if the
weather is warm. Cricket, played over one, four or
five days, is a game that is incomprehensible until
its subtleties have been studied. Then it is glorious,
and enjoyed passionately by its followers.

St John's Wood is the home of Lord's, the holy of
holies for all lovers of cricket. It is the greatest
ambition of any cricketer to perform well at Lord's,
where the game's greatest prize, the Ashes, is kept.
These ashes, preserved in a tiny urn, are fought over
by the Australian and English teams. The tradition
dates back to 1882, the first time Australia ever beat
England on English soil. The following morning a
review of the game appeared in a sporting paper,
saying that English cricket was dead and its body
should be cremated. The following year, England
defeated Australia in a test series 'down under' and
at the moment of victory a young woman ran onto

the pitch, grabbed the bails, and ceremonially burnt them. She placed the ashes in an urn and presented them to England's captain (whom she later married). To this day, the Ashes are fought over each time England and Australia meet in a full test series. No matter which team wins, the Ashes are kept in the Long Room at Lord's.

For two glorious weeks at the end of June and the beginning of July, those lucky few with tickets make their way out to a pleasant southern suburb for the world-famous Wimbledon Lawn Tennis Championships. Of all the tennis courts in the world, Wimbledon's centre court is the most renowned. The turf of this court is used for the annual championship and for nothing else: during the rest of the year it can be seen and admired only from a distance by those visiting the museum. The turf is lovingly tended and brought to a state of readiness by the groundsmen in a way that bears no resemblance to that in which the original turf was laid: the first grass came from the seaside and, as it was laid, ground staff picked shrimps out of it.

For those without tickets, the only way to get into the grounds to watch the tennis is to queue, some hopefuls camping on the pavement overnight to ensure themselves entry the next day. Very occasionally, the weather will have been so bad that 'catch-up' matches are played on the middle Sunday of the tournament. For such occasions no tickets have been pre-sold and much of London's population pours out to Wimbledon to enjoy the feast of tennis on 'People's Sunday'.

ABOVE The Oval, one of London's two main cricket grounds, where international test matches are played each summer. It is also the ground of the Surrey Cricket Club, which was formed in 1844, and county cricket matches are also played here.

RIGHT Lord's Cricket Ground, headquarters of the Marylebone Cricket Club (MCC), the governing body of English cricket since 1788. It is also the county ground of Middlesex. Thomas Lord opened his first ground in Dorset Square in 1787. He moved here in 1814, bringing the original turf with him. The strange flying saucer shaped building suspended over the seating is the NatWest Media Centre, from which radio and television coverage is sent all over the world.

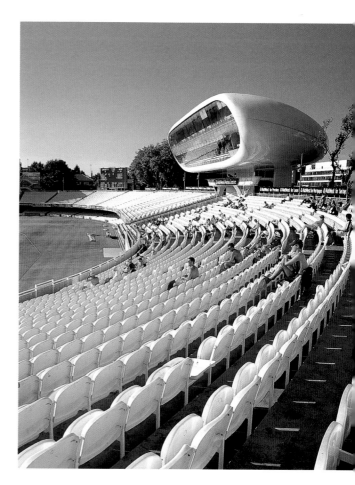

'It is impossible to think of England without its theatre...
...Its theatre still rules the English-speaking world
like the last colonial outpost of an Anglophile empire...'

VANITY FAIR MAGAZINE 1995

The Shadows Lengthen

t the end of the afternoon, workers and visitors again mingle on the streets. The workers, especially in the winter, will be hurrying home, pouring into the Underground and railway stations in a reversal of the morning's activity. But in summer many of them will be tempted to miss the rush hour by popping into a pub for a drink. The pubs are so crowded at 6pm that there is simply no room inside. Instead, people spill out onto the pavement, their laughter loud and carefree.

The Setting Sun

As the sun begins to set over London, exciting shadows are once again created around the fine buildings along the river, causing a myriad reflections on the water. The river takes on an ethereal look. The late sun striking Canada Tower in Canary Wharf is dazzling, transforming the building into a shimmering block of orange or mauve or pink. Downstream, the steel upturned boat-like piers of the Thames Barrier, which has protected the capital from flooding since 1983, are reflected in the rushing water. The barrier is one of the engineering wonders of the modern world. Until it was finished London was in danger of flooding: it was not a case of 'if' London flooded, but 'when'. The cost of constructing the barrier escalated to the huge total of £435 million, but the cost to London if it had not been completed in time would have been unimaginable, as large parts of the capital are underground. Now, if the high spring tide combines with high winds in the North Sea and a tidal wave forces its way up the river, the barrier will close and London will be safe.

The sky is something that is not very obvious in London during the day – it is the buildings that catch the eye – but at sunset, in the parks or along the river, the eye is drawn upwards. In autumn starlings are to be seen as

The 'Mother of Parliaments'
is silhouetted against the
evening sky as the sun sets
over Westminster.

BELOW No. 1 Canada Square is the jewel in the crown of the Canary Wharf development on the Isle of Dogs. At 243 metres (800 feet) high, it is Britain's tallest building, and the second tallest in Europe. It can be seen from the hopfields of Kent to the east and from Hampstead Heath in the north. The stainless steel with which it is clad changes colour as the sun strikes it at different times of day. It is a glamourous office block that has come to be known as 'vertical Fleet Street' because the editorial offices of many of the great daily newspapers, formerly found in the 'street of ink', are now in the Tower.

they gather for their winter migration, forming fantastic patterns high above the heads of the humans who can only watch and marvel at the aerial display.

In the gathering gloom, wolves in London Zoo look out mournfully from behind their bars at the dogs running free in Regent's Park. Then whistles sound and the few remaining joggers, softball players and walkers make their way to the gates and hurry away. As darkness falls, the park is locked for the night and the wolves pace on, silent and alone.

The canals, too, close at sunset. The towpaths are empty, the cyclists hissing quietly along, occasionally ringing their bells to warn of their approach, have all gone, but on the water the occasional narrow boat can still be seen slowly chugging towards its berth for the night.

RIGHT A boat sails serenely through the open Thames Barrier. The barrier, which sits suspended just above the river bed, can be partly or fully raised to control the tidal water. Several times a year, during severe easterly winds and high tides, it is raised completely. Displays in the Visitor Centre explain how it is operated and how it was built.

LEFT The Nags Head pub in Covent Garden. At this time of the day, no pub, however spacious inside, can cope with the number of people seeking liquid refreshment after work, and the pavement is used as an extension of the premises.

ABOVE Little Venice is one of the prettiest parts of London, with very expensive houses flanking the canal. Some people live on the water in narrow boats moored alongside the towpath at night. Here, a last boat makes its way to its overnight mooring as evening falls.

OVERLEAF Dusk over St Paul's and the City. The dramatically lit cathedral, stark against the darkening sky and the myriad reflections of bright lights in the Thames, make this one of the most spectacular views in London.

An Air of Expectancy

In the streets of the West End an excited buzz builds as people scurry about in search of food, or rush back to hotels or homes to change in preparation for the evening's pleasures. In Leicester Square queues of people wait patiently at the Half Price Ticket Booth, hoping to obtain a bargain seat for the show of their choice. Of course, tickets for the really successful musicals will not be found there. For those wanting to see these, the only hope of a last-minute ticket is to wait at the theatre for returns. This is a gamble, for if none materialize it will be too late to find an alternative show.

Much of central London, busy throughout the day, is quieter now. St James's is emptying and so are Oxford Street, Bond Street, the Burlington Arcade and Knightsbridge. All the places in which shops are the *raison d'être* are now becoming still and dark. The City is on its way to becoming a ghost town as the pubs empty and close and the

ABOVE During the day, the great modern office blocks in the City of London reveal nothing of what is being done inside. Now, at dusk, while work continues, their lights go on, and the mysterious goings on behind the plate glass become visible. Soon, though, these lights will be extinguished and the streets of the City will become dark and silent.

RIGHT Trafalgar Square at dusk, and people are looking a little weary. They sit on the edge of the fountains or stand lost in thought while they plan their evenings. The square has a slightly battered look, with a few stray pieces of litter that have escaped the cleaners. In the background, the street lights are ablaze.

RIGHT The London Eye, a spectacular new addition to the London skyline. The Eye was built as part of the millennium celebrations, but if it is a huge success it may remain as a permanent feature. It looks exciting at any time, but at dusk, with Big Ben framed in the centre, it is truly magnificent.

lights are turned off in the banks, insurance houses and commodity exchanges. Elsewhere, the metropolis is waking up, putting on its night face. Bright lights are flashing in a kaleidoscope of colours and shapes. The excitement is building.

London at Night

From Covent Garden in the east to the Hay-market in the west there are over 40 main-stream theatres in central London, and thousands of people come to the capital each year to see its blockbuster musicals, new interpretations of old classics or more intimate reviews. In the narrow streets of Soho and around Piccadilly Circus and Covent Garden, there are hundreds of restaurants serving theatre-goers with pre-show dinners – from the long-established English eating-houses and casual Italian restaurants to the busy Chinese restaurants of Gerrard Street, from the cheap and cheerful to the fashionable and chic – leaving diners ready for the exciting evening of entertainment ahead.

RIGHT The Royal Opera House in Covent Garden is one of the world's premier opera houses, but for years it has been rather shabby, with inadequate facilities both backstage and front of house. Now, after a long closure, the opera house has reopened, magnificently refurbished at vast expense. Its facilities are second to none, and if it can overcome its critics, who claim that it is elitist and out of the reach of ordinary people, 'The House' will be truly a place for all to visit.

LEFT Theatreland, where most of the West End theatres are to be found, is bounded to the south by the Strand. The Vaudeville Theatre is one of several playhouses to be found on this ancient thoroughfare.

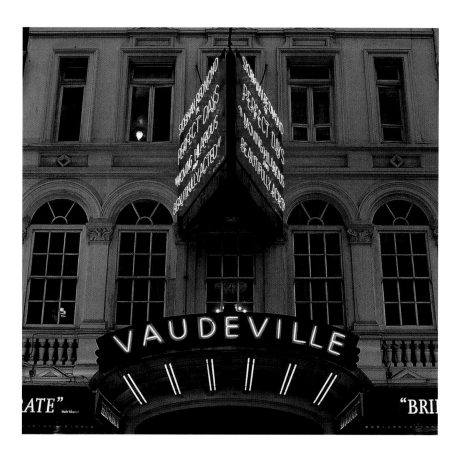

LEFT The Theatre Royal in the Haymarket is the second oldest theatre in London and one of the loveliest. It was designed by John Nash, the Prince Regent's architect, and opened in 1820. The Haymarket, as it is known among theatre folk, has a friendly ghost. He was once the manager of the theatre and, it is said, only appears, beaming happily, if the show is a success!

BELOW The Theatre Royal, Drury Lane, is the oldest theatre in London. There has been a theatre on this site since 1662, when Charles II, on his restoration to the throne, granted two patents for the running of companies of actors. One of these patents was held by Thomas Killigrew, who established the first theatre here. The present building opened in 1812, and today is used mainly for big musicals. Confusingly, the theatre known as 'Drury Lane' is actually in Catherine Street.

Now the pavements of Shaftesbury Avenue are packed with people avoiding ticket touts, making their way into the foyer of their chosen theatre or queuing for last-minute cancellations. Taxis, coaches and private cars draw up outside to disgorge their passengers. Inside the theatre, bells sound to warn latecomers that the performance is about to begin – first three bells, then two, then one. As the last bell sounds, people scurry inside, not to be seen again until the interval, when the street will once more be filled with groups clutching glasses, deep in discussion of the merits of Act One.

In nearby Leicester Square the Odeon Cinema stages major film premières. If there is any chance of a glimpse of the famous – stars of the film, or royal guests – the square is packed with people squeezing against the barriers to get a look at their idols and, if they are lucky, obtain an autograph.

In the City, the Barbican's Concert Hall, like the Royal Festival Hall on the South Bank, is filling with music-lovers. On warm summer evenings concerts can be enjoyed in the idyllic grounds of Kenwood House or Marble Hill House. One of the great highlights of the summer, and billed as the 'biggest live music festival in Europe', is the season of Promenade Concerts – the Proms – which has been held in the Royal Albert Hall since 1941, when their original venue, the

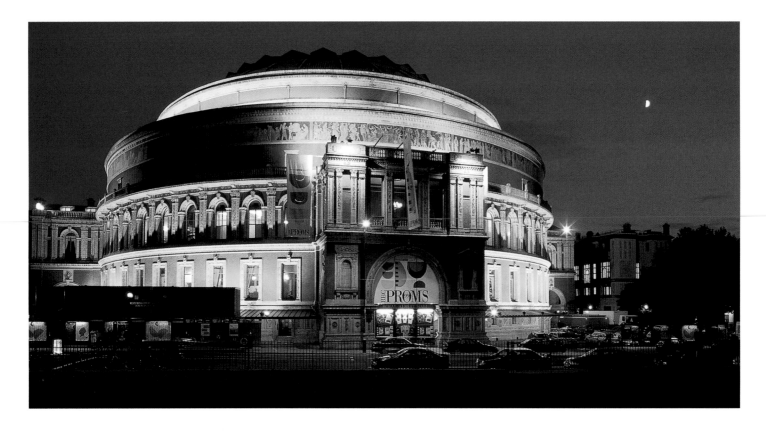

The Royal Albert Hall at night. This fine old domed building with its terracotta frieze illustrating *The Triumph of Art and Letters* was built between 1867 and 1871. Most famous as the venue for 'The Proms', it is also used for public meetings, concerts, balls, tennis tournaments and wrestling matches!

Queen's Hall in Portland Place, was bombed. The Proms were started by Sir Henry Wood in 1895 so that everyone, not just the wealthy, might have access to the finest music. Those who could not afford a seat could, for just a few pence, buy a ticket to stand in the central oval – the 'best value for sixpence in London'. The last night of the Proms is now an institution and many will queue overnight to ensure themselves a place. On the last night the audience participates and the whole boisterous affair, amid enthusiastic flag-waving, is climaxed by the singing of Edward Elgar's 'Land of Hope and Glory'. Elgar always hated the uses to which his *Pomp and Circumstance* march was put, and would probably not approve of this one, but the audience goes out into the night happy and satisfied and determined to do it all over again next year.

On the Fringe

Britain has two world famous theatre companies – the National Theatre and the Royal Shakespeare Company. The National is permanently based on London's South Bank, where it has three theatres within the complex, and the RSC, though based in Stratford-upon-Avon, has a London home at the Barbican. Both companies do pioneering work and their productions can be seen all over the world.

Away from the mainstream, in places like Brixton, Islington, Kilburn and Shepherd's Bush – indeed, all over London – there are 'fringe' theatres. The name comes from the Edinburgh Festival, where there have always been many productions mounted 'on the fringe', in addition to those at the official festival. In London, the Fringe is the equivalent of 'off Broadway' in New York. Some of these little theatres are well established and almost as 'establishment' as the West End itself. A new production at the Almeida in Islington, for example, is reviewed by the top critics of the daily newspapers, while the Hampstead Theatre Club is known to stage interesting new work by important playwrights. But most fringe theatres are less well established and will come and go. Productions are put on in places like pubs and converted church halls, and there is even one theatre

A taxi takes play-goers through Piccadilly Circus to one of the many theatres in Shaftesbury Avenue. It was once the ambition of all British actors to appear 'on Shaftesbury Avenue'. They would serve an apprenticeship in the provinces and then 'stick it out for London' in the hope of seeing their name in lights over the title of a West End success.

in an old mortuary. Some of these venues have only a handful of seats, uncomfortable ones at that, but it is in the fringe theatres that the most exciting new work is produced. Because of the huge expense of mounting a production in the West End, new work is rarely seen there, but is tried out on the Fringe; only when it has proved itself will it be transferred to a major playhouse. So the West End theatres are filled with revivals of popular classics by Oscar Wilde, J. B. Priestley and Pinero, or with sumptuously staged musicals.

Going, Going, Gone

Entertainment of a different kind, but no less dramatic, can be enjoyed in the famous auction houses of London – Christie's and Sotheby's. Most of the sales are daytime events, but the really grand and prestigious auctions, where items change hands for millions of pounds, are held in the evenings: they are black-tie affairs, admission by invitation only, with drinks and canapés served as aperitifs to the main business of the night. The

FROM TOP LEFT Chinatown runs between Shaftesbury Avenue and Leicester Square and is full of restaurants, bakeries and supermarkets selling food that can be found nowhere else in London. The supermarkets of Chinatown are filled not just with Chinese people, but also with rather puzzled-looking would-be chefs searching for ingredients for an oriental feast. Gerrard Street is the main street in Chinatown and the local council has created a pedestrian area with a large entrance gate, special Chinese-style telephone boxes in the shape of pagodas, and street names written in Chinese as well as English. The Chinese people who live and work here come mainly from the New Territories of Hong Kong. This colourful area is at its most lively during the Chinese New Year, when there are dragon dances through the streets and other special entertainments.

BOTTOM RIGHT The Empire Theatre, Leicester Square, is now a cinema, but at the beginning of the 20th century was a theatre that specialised in revues. These entertainments were sumptuously staged and featured beautiful girls, who the 'young men about town' would take out. These 'stage door Johnnies', who would wine and dine the girls and drink champagne from their slippers, along with the whole world of the *demi-monde* that they inhabited, had gone for ever by the end of the First World War.

sense of expectation as a valuable lot comes under the hammer and as the bidding mounts to exhilarating heights makes even the most blasé feel the hairs on the back of their necks stand erect.

A Gastronome's Paradise

For many people, the main business of the evening will be dining out. After the pre-theatre rush, West End restaurants serve more leisurely meals to those who are eating not just because they need fuelling, but because they enjoy good food. There are excellent restaurants all over London serving food from every nation, where world-famous chefs create culinary masterpieces for their discerning clients. The days when London was renowned for the awfulness of its food are long gone.

For a few, the venue itself will be the attraction. Special banquets are now held for specific groups of people in many of London's tourist attractions. Quite the best way of seeing the exhibits in Madame Tussaud's, for example, is to dine surrounded by waxworks of the famous. Dining alongside the skeletons of long-departed species in the Natural History Museum is also an exotic delight!

One of the most exclusive and elegant places for a special dinner or reception is Spencer House, which overlooks Green Park. Here, the visitor can wander freely through eight magnificently restored staterooms and dine in the Great Room,

Those cruising the river by night will be likely to start their journey by passing the Palace of Westminster (left), which is magnificently floodlit. Almost at the other end of their journey, downstream towards Greenwich and the Thames Barrier, they will see the skyscrapers of Canary Wharf (overleaf). Dominant at present is Canada Tower, which needs no floodlighting because it is lit from within. Here, the editorial staff of many of Britain's daily newspapers are hard at work and will remain so long after the cruise ships are safely berthed for the night.

ABOVE The Great Room is the grandest of all the state rooms in Spencer House, which is seen to best advantage at night when all the chandeliers are ablaze. The fine chimneypiece was designed by James 'Athenian' Stuart and has been magnificently copied from the original, now at Althorp, by Dick Reid.

LEFT The dome of St Paul's Cathedral, floodlit at night, is as dominant on the City skyline as it is by day.

where a few years ago the Queen was entertained by all her living prime ministers on the 40th anniversary of her succession to the throne. Spencer House has recently been restored, having languished as office accommodation since the 1920s. It was built by John Spencer, who became the first Earl Spencer and was a direct ancestor of Diana, the late Princess of Wales. It remained the town house of the Spencers until 1924, when they moved out, and from then on it was leased to a number of different companies, who used it as offices. During the Second World War the family removed all the rich interior architectural details

such as door surrounds, skirtings, chair rails and chimney-pieces, in order to protect them from possible bombing. They were taken to Althorp, the country seat of the Spencers, and by the end of the war had been built in there. So when Rothschild Investment Trust Corporate Partnerships (RIT) bought a 125-year lease of Spencer House in 1985 and decided to restore the magnificent staterooms, there was no way that the original pieces could be brought back into the house. The decision was therefore taken to reproduce them using the best materials and employing the finest modern craftsmen. The result is magnificent.

RIGHT Evening along the river. A view looking from the south side across the water to the floodlit Shellmex House flanked to the left by the Adelphi Building and to the right by the Savoy Hotel.

LEFT The climax of a concert in the grounds of Kenwood. Fireworks explode above the stage on the far side of the lake vying with the brightly lit orchestra below for attention. One of the great pleasures for North Londoners on a balmy summer's evening, is to take a bottle of wine and a picnic to the beautiful grounds of Kenwood House, sit on the grass to enjoy the music wafting across the lake and then stroll home across Hampstead Heath.

The Thames is lovely at any time of day, but it has a special mystery at night, and a magical appeal to the visitor. There are a number of boats on which dinner cruises can be taken. The boats glide gently past the floodlit Palace of Westminster, Big Ben, the RAF Memorial, with a glimpse of Nelson's Column in the background, before passing under Waterloo Bridge. Beyond the bridge is the sparkling spire of St Bride, the dome of St Paul's, the City churches, the eerily lit Lloyd's of London and, as the great bulk of HMS *Belfast* looms, the Tower of London and Tower Bridge come into sight. Then on again, past the new Docklands development, to the climax of the cruise – Greenwich, with the delicate little Queen's House nestling between the larger wings of Greenwich Palace. On the way back upstream, after dinner, there is music and dancing. There can surely be no better way of seeing London at night.

The Tower's Ancient History

London's nightlife, in spite of the glittering attractions seen from the river, is centred in the West End. At night the City is like a ghost town, dark and deserted, although on its eastern verges the Tower of London stages an ancient ceremony nightly, watched by just a handful of people who have applied for tickets in advance. The Ceremony of the Keys, as it is known, has been taking place for at least 700 years. Even during the war, when bombs were raining down all around, it was completed every night. On one memorable occasion, when the Tower received a direct hit, the Chief Yeoman Warder was able to report that the ceremony was completed only a little later than usual. In this ancient ceremony, the Yeoman Warder, bearing a brass lantern in one hand and the keys of the Tower in the other, and accompanied by a military escort, locks the West

The Tower of London by night is a romantic sight today, seen from a cruise ship as it sails gently by. In the past this view would have inspired terror. Many of the men who were imprisoned in the Tower were brought to it by river.

Gate, the Middle Tower and the Byward Tower. At the Bloody Tower archway he is challenged by the sentry, who says, 'Who goes there?', and he replies that he brings 'Queen Elizabeth's Keys'. At the end of the ceremony the Chief Warder raises his Tudor bonnet and cries, 'God preserve Queen Elizabeth', and the guard respond, 'Amen', just as

the bell tolls 10pm. A bugler sounds the last post and the Chief Warder goes to the Queen's House and hands the keys to the Resident Governor for safe keeping until the morning. Only those who know the password, which is changed daily, can then enter or leave the Tower.

The evening is drawing to a close and back in

the West End the theatres are disgorging their audiences. People pour out onto the streets, some to go immediately in search of transport home, some to late dining and some to the pubs, which once again are full to bursting. The main entertainment is coming to an end, and for most people bed is beginning to beckon.

London Deserted

After the theatres and concerts finish and 'last orders', then 'time, gentlemen, please', sound in pubs all around London, most people go home to bed and the metropolis empties. By 1am there are few people left, unless you look or listen hard. Then

Select Bibliography

Acknowledgements

BEN WEINREB & CHRISTOPHER HIBBERT
The London Encyclopaedia
Published Macmillan Reference Books 1993

RICHARD TAMES
A Traveller's History of London
Published Interlink Books 1992

ROBERT GRAY
A History of London
Published Hutchinson 1984

F.R. BANKS
The New Penguin Guide to London
Eleventh edition.
Published Penguin 1990

YLVA FRENCH
Blue Guide to London.
Published Black Norton 1998

DAVID PIPER
The companion guide to London.
Published Collins 1985

FRANK ATKINSON
St Paul's and the City.
Published Park Lane Press 1985

DEAN AND CHAPTER OF WESTMINSTER
Westminster Abbey Official Guide
Published Jarrold Publishing1997

EDWARD JONES & CHRISTOPHER WOODWARD
A guide to the architecture of London
New Edition.
Published Weidenfeld & Nicolson 1992

ALAN COX
Docklands in the Making. Survey of London.
Published The Athlone Press for the Royal Commission on
the Historical Monuments
of England 1995

GEOFFREY PARNELL
The Tower of London.
Published BT Batsford Ltd for English Heritage by 1993

JOHN BETJEMAN
The City of London Churches.
Published Pitkin Pictorials Ltd 1985

JOE FRIEDMAN
Inside London.
Published Phaidon Press 1988

AUTHOR

I would like to thank Jo at New Holland for
offering me this commission and Michaella for
helping me to fulfil it. I would like to thank my
son Dan and his wife Sevie, my daughter Kate and
her husband Charlie for encouraging me to take
on this new challenge. I am particularly grateful to
the latter as they read the early drafts and their
comments were of great assistance in shaping the
book. Finally and most importantly, I would like
to thank my husband, Richard Hampton, who
throughout has remained encouraging, patient and
supportive. Richard assisted with the research,
made many helpful suggestions as the work
progressed and fed me regularly when I was faced
with a deadline!

Jenny Oulton

PHOTOGRAPHER

Thanks to all the shopkeepers, market stall-
holders, visitors to and natives of London, who
didn't mind having my lenses pointed at them;
and to Michaella and Jo at New Holland who
remained calm while I was panicking.

David Paterson

the West End the theatres are disgorging their audiences. People pour out onto the streets, some to go immediately in search of transport home, some to late dining and some to the pubs, which once again are full to bursting. The main entertainment is coming to an end, and for most people bed is beginning to beckon.

London Deserted

After the theatres and concerts finish and 'last orders', then 'time, gentlemen, please', sound in pubs all around London, most people go home to bed and the metropolis empties. By 1am there are few people left, unless you look or listen hard. Then

you may be able to discern the regular beat of drums. While most of London sleeps, the pulse of jazz, pop and reggae music is to be found in clubs around the city by those who know where to look.

Among the dark streets of the sleeping capital there are little sunbursts of activity. One of them radiates out from Leicester Square and includes Soho, where those with a mind to, can dance the night away. Further from the centre, Deptford in south-east London attracts students from nearby Goldsmiths College and from Greenwich, while Brixton serves the party-goers of the south-west. In north London, Islington is like a miniature West End and Camden has been made fashionable by the 'Brit pop' bands Blur, Oasis and Suede in recent years. So popular has Camden become, that nearby Primrose Hill is now home to many who work in the media, and the area is full of music studios.

The many late-night venues all over London do not begin their entertainment until well into the evening, but will then continue until two or three the following morning, with the 'headline' band not appearing until around midnight. The excitement builds slowly as the clubs and venues fill up and the supporting bands whip up their audience into a fever of expectation.

This is the London that can be enjoyed by anyone who wants to – where new sounds emerge, and new bands make their first tentative steps towards success. Not too expensive, it is the London of students, of the young and passionate. There are also, of course, the very expensive, exclusive night-clubs frequented by the wealthy – by film- and pop stars. Only members are admitted, and few can gain membership. The same can be said for the clubs frequented by the literati and the intelligentsia. Many Londoners have heard of Groucho's in Soho, but only a few will ever see

The Albert Bridge at Chelsea is one of London's prettiest bridges. It is painted in chocolate box, pastel shades and looks equally delightful by day or by night. Understandably, this view of the bridge at night, is one that is loved by the residents of Chelsea and Battersea – the districts which the bridge connects.

inside it. These are not clubs for the aspiring, but for those who have arrived. Then there are the gambling clubs, some so discreet, looking for all the world like ordinary homes, that it is impossible to imagine that behind their expensively painted front doors, fortunes are made or lost nightly. Try to enter, though, and, unless you are a member, you will be immediately confronted by a uniformed bouncer who will politely, but firmly, send you on your way.

Of course, as in any big city, there are also some people at work. The worlds of the night-worker and the night-reveller are so far apart that they rarely touch. So little do they have in common, that it is as if they are different species. Sometimes, though, those leaving a gig or a drinking club at three or four in the morning will fancy breakfast – and those who have worked all night are also hungry. In Smithfield or Billingsgate, or any of the other wholesale markets, food and drink can be obtained in cafés or pubs and, briefly, party-goers mingle with market porters.

Night-owls of a Different Kind

Despite these pockets of life, an owl flying over London would find most of London asleep and much of the great metropolis in darkness. Only the creatures who hunt through the night are to be found in Hyde Park, Regent's Park or Richmond Park, where the deer move quietly and confidently through the trees. And in Kensington Gardens, the fanciful would say, Peter Pan and the lost boys play all night, while other children sleep. The suburban streets are the domain of the domestic cat, the most placid of moggies reverting to its wild roots at night, when its owners are abed.

Eventually, as the light of a new dawn begins to touch the sky with the faintest of colour, as the birds begin their hesitant first chorus, the thoughts of the ravers, the revellers, the musicians, the gamblers, turn to bed, where they will sleep the day away, awaking refreshed in readiness for the following night's entertainment.

Select Bibliography

Acknowledgements

BEN WEINREB & CHRISTOPHER HIBBERT
The London Encyclopaedia
Published Macmillan Reference Books 1993

RICHARD TAMES
A Traveller's History of London
Published Interlink Books 1992

ROBERT GRAY
A History of London
Published Hutchinson 1984

E.R. BANKS
The New Penguin Guide to London
Eleventh edition.
Published Penguin 1990

YLVA FRENCH
Blue Guide to London.
Published Black Norton 1998

DAVID PIPER
The companion guide to London.
Published Collins 1985

FRANK ATKINSON
St Paul's and the City.
Published Park Lane Press 1985

DEAN AND CHAPTER OF WESTMINSTER
Westminster Abbey Official Guide
Published Jarrold Publishing 1997

EDWARD JONES & CHRISTOPHER WOODWARD
A guide to the architecture of London
New Edition.
Published Weidenfeld & Nicolson 1992

ALAN COX
Docklands in the Making. Survey of London.
Published The Athlone Press for the Royal Commission on
the Historical Monuments
of England 1995

GEOFFREY PARNELL
The Tower of London.
Published BT Batsford Ltd for English Heritage by 1993

JOHN BETJEMAN
The City of London Churches.
Published Pitkin Pictorials Ltd 1985

JOE FRIEDMAN
Inside London.
Published Phaidon Press 1988

AUTHOR
I would like to thank Jo at New Holland for
offering me this commission and Michaella for
helping me to fulfil it. I would like to thank my
son Dan and his wife Sevie, my daughter Kate and
her husband Charlie for encouraging me to take
on this new challenge. I am particularly grateful to
the latter as they read the early drafts and their
comments were of great assistance in shaping the
book. Finally and most importantly, I would like
to thank my husband, Richard Hampton, who
throughout has remained encouraging, patient and
supportive. Richard assisted with the research,
made many helpful suggestions as the work
progressed and fed me regularly when I was faced
with a deadline!

Jenny Oulton

PHOTOGRAPHER
Thanks to all the shopkeepers, market stall-
holders, visitors to and natives of London, who
didn't mind having my lenses pointed at them;
and to Michaella and Jo at New Holland who
remained calm while I was panicking.

David Paterson

Index